BEHAVIOR MODIFICATION

OF LEARNING DISABILITIES

EDITED BY

Robert H. Bradfield

Academic Therapy Publications
San Rafael, California

ISBN: 0-87879-020-9
Library of Congress Catalog
Card Number: 78-169492

1st Printing   1971
2nd Printing   1972
3rd Printing   1974

Printed in the
United States of America

Academic Therapy Publications
San Rafael, California

CONTENTS

III — PROGRAMS IN OPERATION:
Behavior Modification Models and Curriculum in the Classroom
113

CONTRIBUTORS
171

Introduction

I F ONE were to view the emergence of behavior modification theory and practice, and in particular operant theory, on a time continuum, he would find that for all practical purposes the use of the theory is still in its infancy in terms of its application to human behavior. He would also find, however, that its growth rate toward maturity has been just short of phenomenal. The decade of the 1960's has seen a meteoric rise in the use of the principles of learning to alter a wide range of human behaviors, from initial efforts that focused upon the more deviant aspects of human behavior to the more recent emphasis upon normal behavior in the natural environment. In terms of research support for its premises and procedures, behavior theory is today probably more advanced than any other theory of human behavior. It has not simply developed a more sophisticated approach to the analysis and modification of human behavior, but from its inception has provided ongoing, systematic, and detailed analyses that can be replicated, challenged, or subjected to further experimentation. Its greatest strength lies in its own requirement that it lay itself open to investigation and challenge rather than being dependent upon mystical or hypothetical constructs that can never be verified.

This is not to suggest that during the past decade many errors have not been made — they undoubtedly have. In many cases theoretical principles have been misunderstood or misused, and procedures have often been in error. But even when such errors have occurred,

1

a systematic behavioral approach has required that they be made glaringly evident and subject to change and reevaluation. Only in this way can such errors be kept from being perpetuated. No longer must the proponent of behavior theory defend himself against critics for the use of "mechanical" techniques. It has long since been shown that careful behavior modification procedure is, perhaps, the *least* mechanical in its approach, since it must be totally sensitive and must modify its own procedures as a result of change or lack of change in behavior. If the procedure becomes mechanical, it is the direct antithesis of "good" behavior modification. No longer must the proponent of behavior theory defend himself against critics who claim that the procedure is "cold." A careful analysis of a good behavior modification program will show that it requires greater sensitivity and understanding of a human being than any other procedure in existence today. No longer can the question of correct or incorrect value judgments be placed solely in the lap of the behaviorist. There is no question that value judgments must be made, but within the behavior modification framework, at least, value judgments must be clearly stated and must be presented by someone who is responsible for them.

Recently a great hue and cry has arisen with regard to the individual's accountability for his actions, and, in particular, the need for accountability on the part of teachers and school administrators who establish and implement programs for children. This is not a new demand to behavior modifiers. They have made this demand from the beginning. It has always been the position of behavior modifiers that there are no learning failures, only teaching failures, and this requires that teachers be directly accountable for the establishment of programs in which learning does take place, and that they be accountable for the failure of children to learn. This is not to imply that teachers will always have the necessary resources or program capabilities to obtain totally desirable results, nor does it suggest that through behavioral techniques that we can teach a child who has no legs to run a four-minute mile. It does suggest, however, that in an overwhelming majority of instances where children fail to learn, we must recognize that there is something amiss within the learning environment rather than in the child.

This book has been compiled in an attempt to focus the attention of educators and parents upon one of the many categorical program areas currently in existence in education today — Learning Disabilities. Though the definitions of this term today are many and varied, one of the major implications of most such definitions is that some type of neurological deficit or malfunction of the central nervous system of the child exists and has resulted in his inability to learn specific types of academic tasks and social behaviors, to receive correct sensory information, and so forth. Educators have, to date, been somewhat less responsive to the application of behavioral principles to the modification of these disabilities than has been the case in other special education areas.

Needless to say, I have presented in this volume a very general coverage of behavioral procedures that apply to the very complex problem of learning disabilities. It is my hope, however, that the information contained in this brief series will prove exciting enough to cause those who read it to search further. If it can only provide a stimulus that results in a response of using "good" behavioral techniques with learning-disabled children, who knows what positive consequence may result.

Robert H. Bradfield
San Francisco State College

I

General Applications:

BEHAVIOR MODIFICATION

IN EDUCATIONAL AND SOCIAL ENVIRONMENTS

I N THIS SECTION I have included a series of articles that have broad applicability to any program that deals with the education of children, but they are of particular importance to programs that relate to those children who are included within the definition of "learning disabled."

In Chapter 1, Lovitt provides a persuasive argument for the replacement of the traditional "topographical" or individual, isolated diagnostic evaluation procedure with an ongoing, dynamic behavioral assessment that takes place in the natural environment. This kind of assessment includes much more than a simple measure of the child's performance; it must evaluate the behavioral components that may contribute to his performance, along with the contributions of other persons in the environment, namely the teacher and students, as they relate to his performance. This chapter should be of particular interest not only to teachers but to psychologists, physicians, social workers, and other professionals who are involved in the decision-making processes that have tremendous importance for the futures of these children.

In Chapter 2, Wetzel presents a proposal for an administrative design in programs utilizing behavioral techniques. Though he discusses an experimental project that focused upon predelinquent and delinquent children, it will be noted that many of the behaviors designated are frequently encountered in learning-disabled children. In view of its emphasis upon the involvement of all personnel who can become effective behavior modifiers, this chapter should be particularly important to those who are concerned with the establishment of behavioral programs. Wetzel's emphasis upon the use of "teachers, parents, peers, siblings, parole officers, uncles, grocery store owners, and stable managers" at the mediation level requires that we take a much closer look at the use of a wide variety of persons in the natural environment as potential behavior modifiers than we have been inclined to do in the past.

In Chapter 3, I have presented a brief discussion of a Precision Teaching and Management program that will allow teachers, parents, and children to begin to record, change, and manage behavior in a systematic way. This chapter expands, to some extent, on Lovitt's "Assessment of Behavioral Components" section in Chapter 1, while at the same time it attempts to show that a simple and efficient procedure for charting and recording behavior rates, as well as an effective communication system, can become a powerful tool in any ongoing behavioral program.

The final chapter in the first section focuses upon one of the most vital areas of concern in working with learning-disabled children — that of training parents in child management. Bernal discusses programs for the training of parents in the use of behavioral techniques to control the behaviors of antisocial children and presents seven case studies of such procedures.

Chapter 1

Assessment of Children with Learning Disabilities

Thomas C. Lovitt

Reprinted by permission of the author and *Exceptional Children*, December 1967

A REVIEW of the literature on learning disabilities strongly suggests that there is no need for another psychological or medical definition of that population whose achievement does not coincide with its assumed potential. Already there has been as much time expended in attempts to delineate this learning disabilities population as has been spent in its actual diagnosis and treatment. Rather, then, a review of this literature suggests the need for a rationale and a method of evaluation based on a thorough behavioral assessment of individual performance.

Recent concern with learning disorders has prompted not only the publication of books devoted specifically to the diagnosis and remediation of such problems,[1] but also has stimulated an allocation of government funds for the training of professionals in this field. Further, a number of diagnostic centers has been established for the evaluation of children with minimal brain injury or learning disorders.

Characteristically, a diagnosis at these centers involves the formal administration of standardized educational and psychological test batteries, usually including the *Illinois Test of Psycholinguistic Abilities* (ITPA), the *Parsons Language Sample*, the *Detroit Tests of Learning Aptitude*, the *Wepman Auditory Discrimination Test*, and reading measures such as the *Temple University Informal Reading Inventory*, the *Gates-McKillop Diagnostic Reading Tests*, or the *Durrell Analysis of Reading Difficulty*.[2] Following the administration of these tests, portions of which may correlate with the reason for referral, a summary report is presented to the teacher. The tacit assumption behind this diagnostic procedure is that the classroom teacher will be able to translate these evaluations and recommendations into effective programing.

The teacher or referring agent receives (a) such statements as those based upon the ITPA, which reveal the child's auditory decoding and vocal encoding abilities; (b) such data as that obtained from the Parsons Language Sample, which are relevant to his manding, tacting, and intraverbal behaviors; and (c) further comments as to his auditory discrimination, oral reading, comprehension, and phonic abilities. However, these statements are at least one step removed from the direct programing tasks of the referring agent.

For example, there is the teacher who refers a child with an observed deficiency in describing specific objects within the classroom. This teacher will be unable to design a remediation program from a diagnostic report which merely states that, in comparison with someone of his age, the referred child scores poorly on a vocal encoding subtest. This subtest would only be helpful to the teacher were the child referred because of a vocal encoding deficit. Further confusion can result when a teacher actually misuses the indirect information. A teacher, for example, might seek diagnostic solace as a means of rationalizing her own programing inadequacies. Such a teacher, when finding a child who does not adapt to her program or choice of curricular materials, could have her programing decisions greatly reinforced by a diagnostician who solves her dilemma with a report that the child is dyslexic or aphasic. As a result, when the child does not adequately perform, the teacher need only draw out her file and read the diagnosis to reassure herself that the student's poor performance is unalterably determined by some medical or psychological malady. Then, no teaching obligation follows for altering the stimulus or consequence conditions of the program, nor is there any necessity for an assessment of possible errors within the teacher's management techniques.

These difficulties suggest the need for a four-point diagnostic procedure based on a methodological assessment rather than an assessment superimposing a set of population characteristics on an individual child. This four-point procedure is outlined as follows: (a) baseline assessment, (b) assessment of behavioral components, (c) assessment based on referral, and (d) generalization of assessment. In this manner, it is judged, more children displaying discrepant behaviors will be served, for when diagnosis and treatment are based on direct observations and not on the supposition that one deviant behavior presupposes the presence of a syndrome of related events, time is spent in treatment of explicit behaviors rather than in what is frequently a fruitless search for correlate but often unrevealed behaviors.

Baseline Assessment

The proposed diagnostic procedure is initiated by continuously assessing behavior over a period of time, until a specified level of stability has been obtained. This continuous diagnosis is certainly more reliable than traditional diagnostic procedures that represent a single evaluation of behavior or, at most, two samplings of behavior in the pre-posttest paradigm.

In the case where only one or two measures of the behavior are obtained, not only is minimal data acquired, but the total range of variability remains undetected. This minimal evaluative information is often misleading when the objective of a diagnosis is to make a probability statement in regard to the child's future performance. In instances during evaluation when the individual's behavior is under weak or undetected stimulus control, his performance may be extremely variable. The subject, for example, may perform at a very slow rate one day and quite rapidly on another. If only before and after treatment impressions of performance are obtained, the diagnostician cannot be certain if the behavioral change is due to treatment modification or if it is merely fluctuation due to variability.

The diagnostician is concerned not only with the reliability of baseline performance, but also with the validity of his evaluation. In behavioral diagnoses, a valid measure of performance is provided through objective observations of behavior (for example, direct analysis of reading or attention span) rather than subjective inferences of behavior (indirect assessment through the use of standardized tests). Validity, then, obtained from direct measurements that can exactly match recorded observations to those the evaluator will subsequently modify, is assuredly greater than that derived from the indirect sampling of standardized tests that only infer future performance.

Assessment of Behavioral Components

The second aspect of the proposed evaluation process is the assessment of those behavioral components that maintain and modify behavior, such as stimulus or antecedent events, behavioral movements or responses, the contingency system or arrangement of events, and the consequences provided contingent upon a specified behavior.[3]

Antecedent or Stimulus Events. Until recently, most educational researchers have focused on the antecedents of behavior — the stimulus materials presented to children. Their experimental efforts can be seen in the vast amount of research that contrasts the efficiency of one curricular method with another. Although such research provides data meaningful for large groups of children, it does not meaningfully measure the effects of various curricular procedures on individuals. It is suggested that the current high level of concern over individual differences should also extend to an assessment of the effects of the programing of materials on individual performance.

It is quite possible that stimulus or curricular research, with regard to children with learning disabilities, will need to evaluate more discrete aspects of the stimulus process than a mere assessment of various texts, workbooks, slides, or filmstrips. For example, to accelerate or maintain the response behaviors of some children, it may be necessary to analyze experimentally individual preferences for several stimulus dimensions. Many of these preferences can be obtained in a free operant situation: for example, the child selects his preferred rate of visual or aural narration, the intensity or brightness of the aural or visual theme, and/or the configuration or size of the visual stimulus.

Stimulus preferences relevant to the preferred rate of listening are already the object of some research consideration.[4] By continuously listening to a story, at five varying word-per-minute (wpm) rates, retarded and normal subjects were able to select their preferred speed of speech. The results of this investigation revealed that, for most boys, a rather discrete preference for a particular narrative rate did exist. Most normal boys operated to acquire, and verbalized a preference for, speech at normal rates, while all of the retarded subjects in the study rejected the normal 180 wpm rate. Furthermore, they verbalized preferences that were often inconsistent with their operant selections.

A second investigation to assess stimulus preference for the type of person reading a story has recently been completed.[5] Seven preteenage boys from regular and special classes were assessed as to preference for a male or female reader by allowing each boy to listen simultaneously to two recorded versions of a story, one read by a female and the other by a male. In both conditions the story was the same and the wpm rate of speech was nearly identical. Both stories were available throughout the experimental conditions and the boys were provided with a manual device that allowed them to select continuously one reader over the other and to sample portions of both recorded tapes. The results of this study revealed that five of the boys preferred the male reader and one preferred the female reader. One boy's performance indicated that, for him, the reinforcing effects of both readers were nearly the same.

Thus, a programer, supplied with such individually relevant data as preferred rate of narration or preferred type of reader, could design programs based on these or other stimulus dimensions, such as preference of rate and size of visual presentation or timbre and intensity of auditory delivery.

Movement or Response Behaviors. The response behavior of the child with learning disabilities is a second behavioral component that should be assessed. His responses need to be evaluated in regard to both topography (the counting or quantification of responses) and function (the effect of these responses on the environment).

Literature in learning disabilities is abundant in regard to such topographic parameters of language as mean sentence length, type-token ratios, psycholinguistic processes, and manding and tacting behaviors.[6] Other dimensions that could be assessed include speaking rate, timbre of speech, and intensity of speech.

However, as C. B. Ferster has pointed out, topographic analysis is a static measure, while a functional analysis is dynamic.[7] Although a topographic record may be as objective and as easily reproduced as any other datum, it lacks the functional or dynamic relation of the behavior to its controlling environment.

In order to obtain this functional analysis of verbal behavior, it is necessary to assess the many verbal situations in which the deviate or disabled child functions and to determine how often, how long, and by what type of speech the child maintains interpersonal communicative acts. It is necessary also to observe how often he emits vocalizations classified as demands or commands, and the frequency with which these mands are consequated or reinforced.

If modification procedures are based only on such topographic measures as mean sentence length or speech rate, an individual's effect (function) on his environment could remain unchanged. However, by observing behavior within a specific setting and by altering certain topographic elements coincident with this analysis, functional changes may occur. For example, in a situational analysis of language it may be determined that when an individual speaks faster and uses longer sentences he is able to maintain a communicative act longer than when he speaks more slowly and uses shorter phrases. In this instance, if the goal requires longer communicative interactions, procedures would be arranged to modify the person's rate and duration of speech. Only by altering the individual's responses according to such a two dimensional evaluation, which contains sentence length and duration of interpersonal communicative contact, may a functional change be achieved.

Arrangement or Contingency System. The third behavioral component that should be evaluated and assessed is the temporal arrangement of the consequences of behavior. It is necessary to determine how often or how many consequences are necessary to affect performance. Many normal children seem to function with few spuriously dispensed consequences. Most children fulfill teacher expectations even though the consequences of the child behaviors are delivered at irregular and extended intervals. However, these same lean and unsystematic contingencies that maintain acceptable response rates in normal children may be either too subtle or too infrequent to evoke similar behaviors in some exceptional children. Thus, the child described as having an attention span deviation may functionally have a contingency deficit.

H. Kunzelmann et al.,[8] at the Experimental Education Unit of the University of Washington, have designed an observation system that should provide data relevant to the contingency requirements of children. By recording the rate of teacher interactions with individual children and by simultaneously plotting pupil performance rate, data should be obtained relevant to pupil performance as a function of teacher interaction. Data from such a system would enable a class-room teacher to arrange the rate of her interactions to promote optimal pupil response rate. The maintenance of high rates of performance for some children may require few systematically spaced interactions. However, for pupils with contingency deficits, high response rates may be produced only by a high rate of teacher interaction.

Subsequent or Consequent Events. The final behavioral component for measurement and evaluation is the assessment of environmental consequences that maintain behavior. It is necessary to identify an individual's hierarchy of consequences, those events that either increase or decrease his rate of performance. These consequences should be selected so that they coincide with those available in the individual's home or school, and, whenever possible, they should take the form of the complex social consequences that will eventually control the child's behavior in most settings.

Generally there has been more success in determining what these high payoff activities are by observing the child or by asking the child's teacher or his parent, rather than asking the child himself. Parents and teachers are in immediate and close contact with the child many hours each day. They are aware of the child's free time preferences — whether he watches television, builds models, rides his bike, colors in a book, or reads science fiction. These frequently occurring self-initiated activities could be used later by the diagnostician or programer as initial consequences when remediation programs are inaugurated.

The reliability of observation and interview techniques in determining potential reinforcers for children has recently been experimentally analyzed. E. A. Haughton asked teachers, peers, and the children themselves which events or commodities they believed would affect pupil performance.[9] Children were also observed in free time situations, in order to obtain data relevant to potential reinforcers. The suggested and observed events were then used as consequences in an academic setting to determine their relative function on pupil performance. Haughton reported that although some teachers were accurate in predicting which events could be used to increase academic response rate of children, the most reliable information was that data obtained by actually observing the child.

Many instances, however, will arise that require the use of consequences not ordinarily available in a classroom setting, such as tokens, marks, or the classic use of candy, M&M's.[10] With some children it may even be necessary to explore the use of continuous narration (such as stories or music) as a potential controlling consequence. It could be that such continuously available narration will generate higher rates of response from those individuals than will bursts or episodes of reinforcement, such as tokens, marks, or social contacts.

Another approach is the method of conjugate assessment, which requires that a child be placed in an enclosed room and told that he will be listening to or looking at something and that he can press the provided hand switch if he so desires. Without further instructions, the child usually realizes that by pressing or not pressing the switch he can continuously select the narration of his choice. Since many children with learning disabilities possess limited verbal repertoires, this free operant technique, which requires minimal verbalization from the examiner and none from the child, obtains a more reliable assessment than those requiring a verbal report from the child.

The conjugate tactic has been used to compare the continuous reinforcing strengths of five types of narration, [11] and to compare the relative reinforcing strengths of two stories. [12] In the first investigation, when a story, a poem, words and sentences in reverse order, and a journal article were serially presented, it was observed that young children responded at stable rates to acquire the story, but they demonstrated great response variability when the other narrations were programed. Some exceptional children, however, responded at more stable rates to acquire words or sentences in reverse order than they did for the story, a narrative form that was conceivably understood or meaningful.

In the second investigation of the comparative strengths of consequences, [13] two stories were offered simultaneously rather than serially. The data from this study not only revealed each subject's quantitative preference for a story, but also provided a continuous, moment to moment analysis of the holding power of each story.

Assessment Based on Referral

The third factor which must be considered in this recommended evaluation process is the referring agent — the teacher or parent — as well as the referred child. The possibility always exists that the managerial and programing skills of the adult may be as incompetent as the compliance skills of the child. In other words, there are those educators and psychologists who, given an option as to program types, would select the program for adults with programing disabilities, rather than one for children with learning disabilities. In some cases, it is expedient for the diagnostician to deal directly with the programing disability of the adult rather than with the performing disability of the child.

Involving a parent or teacher in the evaluation process enables the referring agent to collaborate with the diagnostician on the determination of target behaviors specified for subsequent treatment. It would not be uncommon to find a child referred and diagnosed because of poor performance in oral and silent reading, inadequate mathematics computation, and other discrepant activities such as tantrums or social isolate behavior. In this case the deviant behaviors need to be ranked by priority — a rank order not necessarily in accord with the diagnostician's treatment sequence. Such a decision should be mutually agreed upon by the diagnostician and referring agent.

Although the diagnostician sometimes runs the risk of reinforcing the referring agent's poor judgment and analysis by allowing her to play a role in deciding the future course of educational treatment and modification, there are indications that a breakdown in programing results from the failure to take the referring agent's goals into account. On some occasions, when a disagreement in terminal goals results in dual programing, either the child becomes adept at discerning inconsistent environment expectations or his behavior collapses completely. On other occasions, a parent may verbalize agreement but fail to carry out any modification procedures as outlined by the diagnostician. For the optimal programing sequence, then, a coincidence of goals held by the adults must be actively pursued.

Generalization of Assessment

The fourth aspect of the proposed method of assessment is to emphasize the generalization of diagnostic information. The end product of an evaluation should be to present to the referring agent information that can be immediately transmitted into programing procedures. The teacher, when provided with diagnostic information from the clinician, should be in a position to provide a stable learning environment for the referred child.

One reason for the fact that diagnostic information has not been translated into academic programs has been discussed earlier, namely that teachers have not always been able to design functional teaching programs and procedures from the data derived from standardized tests and the accompanying clinical jargon. A second reason that clinical evaluations fail to result in functional academic programs may be that the environmental conditions that prevailed during evaluation were not specified to the teacher. It is as important to report the process that was in operation during an evaluation as it is to report the product of an assessment. An evaluation report that simply states the child's rate of response on certain materials would be a topographic analysis. However, an assessment report that not only describes the child's performance rate, but details the environmental contingencies that were in effect during assessment, would be a functional analysis. The probability of successfully generalizing a remediation program is far greater when functional data are provided than when only topographic information is reported.

Attempts are being made at the Experimental Education Unit and Division of Child Health of the University of Washington to report diagnostic data to teachers in a functional manner.[14] Data are reported which are relevant to each of the following: the antecedent prompts or instructions given during the evaluation, the exact material that was given the performer, the subsequent events that followed the child's responses, and the child's responses to the various programs. The assessment of explicit academic behaviors and the reporting of prevailing environmental conditions have facilitated diagnostic generalization. Thus, diagnostic generalization can be obtained when data are reported relevant to process and product rather than product alone.

Conclusion

The concern throughout this paper has been directed toward assessment. Although treatment or remediation was not the emphasis at this time, this detailed method of objective specification and direct observation of behavior which has actually been established by the teacher or diagnostician represents the first step toward successful modification.

The utilization of direct behavioral assessment as an initial step toward future teaching plans carries with it both optimism and a high degree of responsibility. Optimism is implied in that the discovery within a detailed behavioral analysis of those conditions that alter or maintain behavior may lead to the alteration of many deviant behaviors. There is no need to seek a validation of the referred behavior from some indirect or irrelevant standardized test. Furthermore, there is no need to probe for hidden behaviors that are often suspiciously believed to be correlated with the referred behavior. Responsibility is implied in that now the remediational obligation rests with the programer. For when remediation procedures are initiated and accordingly measured in a direct manner but resulting pupil responses are unacceptable, it is indicated that the variables in a teaching situation have not been appropriately arranged. Therefore, the ultimate successes and failures of the proposed assessment and modification method are always subject to immediate and accurate observation. By direct assessment of such behaviors as rates of reading, computation, or listening and speaking, and by the application of modification procedures functionally related to these skills, pupil and/or programer progress is discerned immediately and empirically.

NOTES

1. J. Hellmuth (ed.), *Learning Disorders*, Vol. 1 (Seattle, Wash.: Special Child Publications, 1965); E. C. Frierson and W. B. Barbe (eds.), *Educating Children with Learning Disabilities: Selected Readings* (New York, N.Y.: Appleton-Century-Crofts, 1967).

2. For sources of tests mentioned in this article, see References.

3. O. R. Lindsley, "Direct Measurement and Prosthesis of Retarded Behavior," *Journal of Education*, 147 (1964), 62-81.

4. T. C. Lovitt, "Narrative Rate Preference of Normal and Retarded Males as Assessed by Conjugate Reinforcement." Unpublished doctoral dissertation (Lawrence, Kans.: University of Kansas, 1966).

5. T. C. Lovitt, "Reader Preference: A Free-operant Assessment." Unpublished manuscript (Seattle, Wash.: University of Washington, 1967).

6. J. E. Spradlin, "Language and Communication of Mental Defectives," *Handbook of Mental Deficiency*, ed. N. R. Ellis (New York, N.Y.: McGraw-Hill, 1963), pp. 512-555.

7. C. B. Ferster, "Classification of Behavioral Pathology," *Research in Behavior Modification*, eds. L. Krasner and L. Ullmann (New York, N.Y.: Holt, Rinehart and Winston, 1967), pp. 6-26.

8. H. Kunzelmann et al., "Simultaneous Cumulative Observation Record for Interaction Analysis." Unpublished manuscript (Seattle, Wash.: University of Washington, 1967).

9. E. A. Haughton, "A Practical Way of Individually Tailoring Classroom Consequences." Unpublished doctoral dissertation (Lawrence, Kans.: University of Kansas, 1967).

10. N. G. Haring and T. C. Lovitt, "Operant Methodology and Educational Technology in Special Education," *Methods in Special Education*, eds. N. G. Haring and R. L. Schiefelbush (New York, N.Y.: McGraw-Hill, 1967), pp. 12-48.

11. T. C. Lovitt, "Use of Conjugate Reinforcement to Evaluate the Relative Reinforcing Effects of Various Narrative Forms," *Journal of Experimental Child Psychology*, 5 (1967), 164-171.

12. T. C. Lovitt, "Free-operant Preference for One of Two Stories: A Methodological Note," *Journal of Educational Psychology*, 58 (1967), 84-87.

13. Ibid.

14. T. C. Lovitt and J. D. Kidder, "Experimental Analysis of Children with Learning Disabilities," *Prospectives in Contemporary Education*, ed. R. C. Jones (New York, N.Y.: Allyn and Bacon, in press).

REFERENCES

Baker, Harry J., and Bernice Leland. *Detroit Tests of Learning Aptitude.* Cincinnati, Ohio: Public School Publishing Co., 1935-55.

Cawley, Jack. *Temple University Informal Reading Inventory.* Philadelphia, Pa.: Temple University, 1960.

Durrell, Donald D. *Durrell Analysis of Reading Difficulty.* New York, N.Y.: Harcourt, Brace & World, 1955.

Gates, Arthur I., and S. McKillop. *Gates-McKillop Diagnostic Reading Tests.* New York, N.Y.: Bureau of Publications, Teachers College, Columbia University, 1962.

Kirk, Samuel A., James J. McCarthy and Winifred Kirk. *Illinois Test of Psycholinguistic Abilities (ITPA).* Urbana, Ill.: University of Illinois Press, 1968, revised.

Spradlin, Joseph. *Parsons Language Sample.* Unpublished test. Parsons, Kans.: Parsons State Hospital and Training Center, 1960.

Wepman, Joseph. *Wepman Auditory Discrimination Test.* Chicago, Ill.: Language Research Associates, 1958.

Chapter 2

Therapeutic Engineering in the Natural Environment

Ralph J. Wetzel

RELIANCE ON BEHAVIOR modification principles holds important implications for organization and reorganization of mental health and educational programs. For the past three years my colleagues and I have been exploring some of these implications. Aided by a grant from the Office of Juvenile Delinquency and Youth Development, Dr. Roland Tharp, Dr. Gaylord Thorne and I organized the Behavioral Research Project which operated out of the Southern Arizona Mental Health Center in Tucson. Dr. Tharp was the director of the Psychology Department at the Center, and Dr. Thorne was the project's executive director. For two years the Behavioral Research Project, using assorted tools of behavior modification and contingency management, attempted to modify a variety of so-called predelinquent behaviors in 112 children, ages six through sixteen. This group of children, predominantly Anglo- and Mexican-American, represented grades one through eleven in Tucson Public Schools, with IQ's from below 89 to 149, and with parental occupations ranging from professionals to unskilled laborers.

From these 112 children, the Behavioral Research Project collected records, mostly cumulative records, of 160 discrete behaviors, among which were the following:

- *Disruptive behavior*: out of seat, inappropriate classroom noises, throwing objects, etc.

- *Appropriate academic behavior*: finishing assignment, dressing out for gym, etc.
- *Truancy and tardiness*.
- *Stealing*: from parents and school lockers.
- *Property destruction*: fire setting, destroying family car, etc.
- *Bed wetting and soiling*.
- *Chores*: mowing lawn, taking out garbage, cleaning horse corral, etc.
- *Fighting, defiance*: obscene language, tantrums, etc.

Because we believed that the environment controls most predelinquent behavior, we attempted to work in the natural environment where reinforcers can be found which do indeed alter the behaviors of children. These reinforcers are in the hands of those who have natural, powerful, role relationships to the child: parents, teachers, siblings, peers, and employers. It is in the world of these relationships that our project operated. We declined to see the target child ourselves. All our management attempts were mediated by those individuals who had these kinds of relationships to the problem child.

I shall not detail here what happened. The report of contingency management and what really happens to human behavior is itself a complicated endeavor. We are encouraged by what happened. Predelinquent behaviors can be significantly reduced by a program of behavior modification in the natural environment — of that we have no remaining doubt. Though we were reinforced by the achievement, it is still only an approximation to the ultimate criterion. The technical aspects of the operation were confounding in complexity, and part of my concern in this paper is to reveal some of our experience with the logistics of such an enterprise. Hence, the title, *Therapeutic Engineering in the Natural Environment*. It is, perhaps, a bit euphemistic and equivocal as a title. *Engineering* suggests a degree of precision in management, which I doubt we had in most cases. Some use the term *intervention*, while others regard the process to be little more than meddling in someone else's affairs. I would opt for the term *consultation* as a process of therapeutic engineering. In this paper I will examine some of the ideas upon which these concepts were based as we conducted our project.

WE NEED NOT ARGUE at this point whether or not human behavior is controlled by reinforcement contingencies. Enough data have been generated to warrant the conclusion that properly engineered contingencies will result in significant changes in human behavior. In this endeavor, the contingency (the relationships between one or more behaviors and the environment) may be the most precisely understood element. Implementing or establishing the contingency, however, may be a very complex matter indeed. It is to this latter process that I am directing the term *consultation*.

No organized attempt to alter human behavior is without continual confrontation by the fact that the environment in which the individual is embedded is principally responsible for the organization or disorganization, the maintenance or change, the appearance or disappearance of almost any normal or abnormal behavior with which we are concerned. There is growing realization that the professional relationship is severely limited in its ability to modify behavior if there is no change of conditions in the natural environment of the target (i.e., the subject, client, student, or patient). Reflected in many new community and institutional programs is a growing willingness to enter into the real world of the individual and to seek therapeutic reorganization there.

Many of us who are involved in such programs have grown quite adroit at pointing out the shortcomings of the traditional techniques of behavior change and treatment. The illness-disease medical model has been oft and thoroughly attacked and criticized, as have the intrapsychic theories and the treatment techniques based upon them. But though most of us are agreed that the real power for change lies in the natural environment, our own power to change that environment has been less than we would wish. The helping and educating professions are being called upon to focus intervention in the environment of the individual when our tradition has practically ignored it. We lack both a theoretical orientation and a model for professional organization that lend themselves to the involvement of the broader community and natural relationships in behavior change. This is true both in mental health and education.

It is clear that any procedure that relies upon the environment of an individual to be the agent of behavioral change must be able to organize its essential controlling agents, and if we are to harness the great power, which we suspect lies in natural relationships, we must be able to inform the participants. Here, perhaps, is the weakest element in contemporary practice: *we by and large do not know what to tell people to do.* We lack both data and theoretical principles on which to base clearcut recommendation to parents, teachers, siblings, peers, spouses, employers, and clients. There has developed, in fact, in many therapeutic and consulting procedures, a strong prohibition against giving direct advice concerning action and management. There are several available theoretical rationales for this, but I suspect the probable one may be that no techniques of consultation produce a trusted outcome. The net result is passivity in consultant behavior, whether he be therapist, social worker, minister, teacher, or consulting psychologist. We are ill-prepared indeed to begin helping people in natural relationships to assume a role in behavioral reorganization of target individuals. Our efforts to persuade, cajole, educate, or otherwise influence a target's significant others is often a frustrating and short-lived accomplishment. The task before us is to develop the much-needed techniques of working with the broader environment in training, supervision, and general management. Professions charged with behavioral change must do more than reproduce themselves. They must evolve new theory and new organization.

OUT OF THE CONTEMPORARY work of the so-called behavior modifiers, several working models of consultation have begun to emerge, and they should be mentioned here because they define the principle considerations involved in therapeutic consultation. The work of Ayllon and his colleagues is a nice starting point.[1] These workers set out to demonstrate that the frequency of psychotic behavior could be reduced and the frequency of more appropriate behaviors increased through the management of reinforcement contingencies as they were administered by ward staff and psychiatric nurses. Their work has shown that psychotic behavior is modifiable through the management of reinforcement contingencies. Ayllon also reported in some detail on the process and rationale by which he consulted to ward staff. The following inferences may be made from Ayllon's work in an effort to summarize some of the essential concerns of therapeutic consultation: (1) ward staff were chosen to be the agents of change because they controlled the available patient reinforcers; (2) the ward staff determined the target behaviors because the experimenter-consultants had no authority over the ward staff or within the administrative system; (3) data collection procedures were difficult to maintain because they were not reinforcing to the staff; (4) ward personnel were trained in a few general reinforcement principles but were also told specifically what to do, e.g., "During this program the patient must not be given attention for her psychotic talk about her illegitimate child and the men chasing her. Check the patient every thirty minutes and (a) tally for psychotic talk; and (b) reinforce (and tally) sensible talk." (This is very direct advice indeed.) (5) Ward personnel were monitored in direct observation and supervision; (6) new personnel required a constant training program.

There are other reports which indicate some problems and some techniques, as well as some of the issues, involved in therapeutic reorganization. Burchard and Tyler report on the effects of the staff meeting on the recording and contingency management behavior of cottage personnel in an institution for juvenile boys.[2] I have reported the training procedures and rationales of consultation to a children's institution in which the Mexican cook was the primary agent of therapeutic behavioral change.[3] The cook required only twenty minutes of instruction. Wolf, Risley and Meese report on a consulting process to a children's psychiatric ward staff.[4] This study, in my opinion, is destined to become a classic in technique of consultation to the natural environment. After the ward staff was trained in behavioral management techniques, they in turn began to consult to and train the parents of the target subject by bringing the parents to the ward for supervision, making home visits, and gradually extending behavioral control to them. Parents were also involved in the data collection procedures. The authors apparently worked infrequently with the target and his parents, spending most of their time with the ward attendants, who in turn became the therapeutic agents and consultants to the parents. It is a very nice model of dispersion of therapeutic effectiveness.

Other studies, such as Whaler's,[5] or some of our own work with parents of behaviorally disturbed children or teachers of problem children,[6] suggest other techniques by which therapeutic effectiveness can be dispersed into the natural environment. This is not meant to be a review of behavior modification literature. The point is that one can find imbedded in the behavior modification literature the beginnings of a theoretical rationale and technique for consultation and/or therapeutic engineering in the natural environment.

I SHOULD LIKE to return now to a discussion of our Behavioral Research Project and describe the organization and the process of operation. They both derive from the preceding considerations. We begin with a few questions: What would the helping professions look like if we really believed that behavior is a function of the environment? How would we organize, for instance, a community mental health center, if we believed that the most effective point of intervention is in the contingencies between behavior and events in the surrounding milieu? Behavior modification usually requires the establishment of contingencies and their maintenance. This frequently takes the form of telling particular people in the target's environment what to do and making sure that they do it. How shall we organize toward this aim?

Project Organization

In the Behavioral Research Project, modification of target behavior in predelinquent children required three levels of functional organization. These functions are requisite to any large scale application of behavior modification techniques, both in the helping and in the educating professions. First is a *directing and decision making function*. At this level, decisions are made about the specific technique to be used in the modification of a given behavior in the repertoire of a given individual. The process by which a given program is to be monitored and data collected on its effectiveness is established. In short, it is at this level that the system of behavioral intervention is designed. In the Behavior Research Project the personnel at this level consisted of three Ph.D. psychologists. This is not the least bit necessary. Anyone who can design a system of behavioral intervention and a process for monitoring and evaluating will do. In our opinion, it requires a knowledge of learning principles, behavior modification techniques, and principles of research design. This is the behavior modifier level, the level occupied by Ayllon and by Wolf, Risley, and Mees in their respective studies.[7] It is the primary level of consultation.

The second function is that of *coordination and liaison* between the designers and the environment of the target. This was the fulcrum of our project. Specific information about the target's particular repertoire and his environment must be transmitted to the directing level. Likewise, when an intervention plan is devised, the requisite directions must be carried back to the environment and implemented. This is the secondary level of consultation. Further, the intervention must be monitored, and data on the success or failure of a design must be brought back for evaluation, so that the program may be readjusted if necessary.

At the beginning, it was not clear what skills this level required, since no such job description exists in the helping professions. We sought people who were interested in mental health work, particularly in work with children. We looked for combinations of intelligence and personality that would allow for a good deal of role flexibility, assumption of responsibility, the capacity to relate objectively but in a friendly manner, and above average frustration tolerance. We avoided anyone who had already had experience in a mental health setting, or who was committed to a psychodynamic approach to helping children. Six persons with bachelor of arts degrees were hired.

We originally hired these people under the job title of "case aide," but when they later objected to the bedpan sound of this title, we changed it to "behavioral analyst." They were a varied group. The oldest was a man, about fifty years of age, with a degree in sociology. He spoke fluent Spanish and had intimate knowledge and understanding of the Tucson Mexican-American culture. He had spent his life in a variety of occupations, including carpentry and longshoring. Three young females, recent bachelor of arts graduates from the University of Arizona, were also hired. Their degrees were in sociology, psychology, and public administration. A housewife in her early thirties, with a background in education, and a Negro male who majored in art and had been right guard on the University football squad, rounded out our cadre of behavioral analysts.

We trained the behavioral analysts for six weeks in a didactic, intense, "brainwashing" fashion in principles of learning, behavior modification techniques, and data collection and analysis. Several discussions on ethical and philosophical considerations also evolved. Training and supervision, of course, continued with the beginning of the first case work.

I cannot overemphasize the importance of this role in the organization of the helping professions around behavior modification principles. Our group has become remarkably resourceful and has developed in the past two years behavior modification skills in their own right. The amount of direct supervision has become considerably reduced. These individuals represent a source of manpower not frequently tapped by the professions: the B.A. graduate. Who the personnel at this level are, of course, is not the prime consideration; it is, rather, that the functions of coordination and liaison are essential to the application of behavioral principles. The role requires people who can maintain contacts with the broader community and who understand the rationales and requisites of behavior modification work. We have worked with public health nurses, probation officers, teachers, and social workers in the same functional capacity.

The third functional level is the organization and maintenance of stimulus events and reinforcement contingencies around the target behaviors. In the model I am describing here, this function is carried by people in the environment of the target child who naturally arrange stimulus events and dispense reinforcers. They include teachers, parents, peers, siblings, parole officers, uncles, grocery store owners, and stable managers. They have two common characteristics: they control reinforcing events of functional value to the target, and they are willing to dispense the reinforcers in a contingent fashion. We labeled these individuals the *mediators*, since their function is to mediate between reinforcing events and target behaviors.

This, then, is the basic organization of the Behavioral Research Project. It requires the involvement of three groups — *supervisors, behavioral analysts*, and *mediators* — which have three respective functions: intervention design and supervision at one level, coordination and liaison at another, and contingency management at the third. The functions are important — who fills them, highly variable.

Project Operation

The operation is a system of information flow in which instructions concerning behavioral management move from the directive to the mediator level, while data on the effectiveness of a technique move from the mediator to the directive level. To illustrate the operational sequence, we will consider an example target: let us say that a junior high school principal calls and reports that a pupil has been using obscene language, been defiant in the classroom, and is suspected of stealing. The first operational step is to secure *permission*. The behavioral analyst goes to the home, explains what the project is and does, and secures written permission to work in the situation.

Step two is an information gathering operation. In the school, teacher's lounge, home, and other relevant locales, the behavioral analyst interviews various mediators to determine such matters as the precise nature and circumstances of the complaint behaviors, their approximate frequencies, acceptable alternatives, the existing contingencies, potential reinforcers, the available mediators, and an estimate of mediator willingness to consequate. To survey potential reinforcers, we make an exception to our general procedure of not seeing the child. We ask a tester (usually a psychology graduate student from the University) to see the child. Using a structured interview situation (a sentence-completion test we are working on), and a modified version of the *Thematic Apperception Test*,[8] the interviewer attempts to get as good an idea as he can about the functional reinforcers for the child. (What he likes — doesn't like, does — doesn't do, approaches — avoids, etc.) The interviewer ranks these subjectively.

The following is an illustration of this information-gathering process. The behavioral analyst in the case of the referred junior high student obtained descriptions of obscene language from the teachers (what was said, in which classes, how often, to whom, under what circumstances, and with what consequences). The same descriptions were obtained for disruptive behavior. The rate of truancy over the previous two months was charted from school records. Stealing in this particular case was dropped as a target behavior, since investigation produced no evidence. The parents' complaints about the child's failures to do chores and come home on time were similarly detailed.

Step three is measuring the baseline frequencies against which comparisons are made for program effectiveness. The behavioral analyst prepares an appropriate recording form for the mediator to use in observing and recording complaint behaviors. The success at baseline recording is highly variable. It is hazardous at best, at least in our work. Sometimes, of course, if the behaviors endanger self or others — fire setting, for example — the baseline cannot be be observed. Sometimes the environment is unwilling to wait. Sometimes behavioral analysts put intervention contingent on baselines. We have some quite adequate baselines, some that are not so effective, and there are many behaviors on which we have none at all. It is a very important area for further work. In the case of the junior high student, the teacher was willing to mark the occurrence, per quarter-day-intervals, of one or more uses of obscene language and of predefined defiant acts. The child's mother recorded whether or not chores were completed within fifteen minutes of instruction and the number of minutes he was late in returning home in the evening.

Step four is the intervention plan. (These operations are not as linear in execution as they appear here. Parts of these various steps tend to occur simultaneously.) The analyst consults with the supervisor to formulate an intervention plan. The basic form is always the same: instruct the mediators so that the environment declines to reward misbehavior and rather simultaneously rewards approximations to desired behavior. There seem to be infinite combinations of mediators, reinforcers, and contingencies for arranging more fortunate and therapeutic systems for most targets. Availability of mediators and reinforcers, cost, ease of monitoring, and many other factors enter into the initial design. In this student example, the list of reinforcers included football practice, money, TV, and helping father at the gas station on the weekends. The initial plan was as follows: if the target appeared in and remained in all classes, he could play football after school. Although this may seem straightforward enough, it was a tough contingency to implement. The coach was interested in and willing to make football practice contingent on class attendance. However, he was not willing to run around the school every afternoon trying to find out if the target had been in his classes or not. For the first three days of intervention in this case, the analyst had to go to the school at dismissal time, check with all teachers, and run down to the field to give the coach the high sign. Finally, the school attendance officer agreed to pull the target's attendance record early and report it to the coach; consequently, the system was operated entirely within the school by school personnel.

A point-system of reinforcement was used with the target. He earned points by beginning assignments when instructed and "working steadily" as defined by the teacher. The more steady the work, and the less he talked unnecessarily or obscenely, and without defiance, the more points. A point scale was arranged so that every five points earned produced one-half hour of TV at home. Every ten points earned one hour in the gas station on Saturday. The analyst typed several slips of paper on which the teacher entered the points and his or her signature. These notes were brought home daily where they were accumulated, reinforced, exchanged, and charted according to analyst instructions.

IN GENERAL, an intervention plan resembles many studies of behavior modification found in the literature. We have generated a variety of intervention techniques. The behavior analyst monitors the system, tells mediators what to do, say, and when to do it. He prepares record charts and instructs the mediators in their use; collects records; calls and visits to make sure that contingencies are being maintained; modifies the system as needed in consultation with the supervisor; and works towards establishing self-maintaining systems. We have had some very successful and interesting cases. Our analysts demonstrated an unpredicted amount of talent for devising contingencies and maintenance systems. We also have had some colossal failures. Some systems never got off the ground. However, there are at least two positive aspects of our failures. One is that when we failed, we usually had a reasonably clear idea of why. The other is that we never increased the frequency of a complaint behavior.

The theoretical model of consultation emerging from this experience is one in which each level of operation establishes and maintains a contingency with specific behaviors at the next level. Supervisors shape and maintain behavior analyst behavior with such reinforcers as praise, attention, and money. Behavior analysts reinforce mediators with attention and potential relief from aversive target behaviors. Mediators reinforce targets with available functional reinforcers. At each level, target behaviors and reinforcement contingencies must be clear. In general we work toward a system in which mediators and targets can become mutually reinforcing, thus allowing for behavior analyst withdrawal.

THE PROJECT that I have described here is a rough attempt to explore the implications of behavior modification principles for the helping and educating professions. There are varieties of resistance to the changes in theory and organization that the behavioral approach suggests, and these arise from many sources. Many mediators are revolted by the deterministic philosophy. Others, clinging to a sort of "Protestant ethic" object to rewarding a child for behaviors that he "should" already be producing. We were criticized by our mental health colleagues for treating symptoms rather than causes. There is one source of resistance, however, which is not so clearly identified, but which is most effective in preventing change. One reason why it is not easily identified is that it often appears to support new ideas while preventing attempts to implement them. For lack of a better name, I shall call this source of resistance "the establishment." It is not only, or even necessarily, individuals. It is the organization itself, the rules, the habits, and traditions that often keep a program static, even when all members desire change. The structure of service organizations is usually designed for reasons other than establishing contingencies for the *individuals* who are being served. Thus the staff, line and communication patterns in schools and mental health centers are not oriented to the particular needs of an individual student or patient. The staff tends to be organized around staff needs. Many of the intervention operations we suggested were seen as structurally impossible. For example, it was difficult in the football contingency to move information on desirable behavior, either within the school or between school and home. Schools are geared to widespread transmission of information about undesirable behavior but have no facility for reporting the occurrence of desired behavior.

Another characteristic of the mental health and education establishments is that the principle functions are regarded to be highly professional matters closely managed by a relatively small group of professional people. If we regard the mental health field to be among the "helping professions," then the process of helping (treatment) is regarded to be a professional matter. In a sense we are a culture in which can be found a few highly paid, highly trained "helpers." These helpers maintain, of course, that nonprofessionals are not capable of helping and, in fact, are likely to do harm if they try. Most parents and teachers see no positive role for themselves in helping their behaviorally disturbed child. The same attitude of professionalism exists in education. Many teachers and administrators behave as though only school personnel were capable of teaching a child. Parents are cautioned to be parents and to let the teachers teach. Only a few teachers consider that parents or classroom peers are capable of teaching, and only a handful use them.

This professionalism of the establishments is one of the strongest sources of resistance to change that is based on behavior modification principles. In part, this is because behavior modification techniques tend to "deprofessionalize" the helping and education functions and disperse them into the broader environment. In the Behavioral Research Project, we have found that parents, teachers, and others can become effective therapeutic agents. Schools have never tapped systematically the potentials that parents, peers and others have as agents in the educative process. When we consider the jurisdictional disputes that arise *within* the professions today, we can imagine the resistance to a deprofessionalization process.

Mental health workers and teachers need not fear that they will be separated from their professions nor that their work will fall into the hands of unskilled laymen, if the broader environment is utilized. They will, in fact, have greater responsibility as managers and designers of whole helping and educating systems. But their roles *would change*, and changes are usually resisted.

There are other implications of behavior modification techniques for the professional organization: decentralization of effort out of institutions, and changes in architecture and philosophy. We must look at these implications and realize that these new concepts do not fit well into old organization patterns. Only by exploring new professional organization systems can we effectively use the great resources in the natural environment for two of our most respected human efforts: helping and teaching.

NOTES

1. T. Ayllon and J. Michael, "The Psychiatric Nurse as a Behavioral Engineer," *Journal of the Experimental Analysis of Behavior*, 2 (1959), 323-334.

2. J. Burchard and V. Tyler, Jr., "The Modification of Delinquent Behavior through Operant Conditioning," *Behavior Research and Therapy*, 2 (1965), 245-250.

3. R. J. Wetzel, "Use of Behavioral Techniques in a Case of Compulsive Stealing," *Journal of Consulting Psychology*, 30 (1966), 367-374.

4. M. M. Wolf, T. Risley, and H. Mees, "Application of Operant Conditioning Procedures to the Behavior Problems of an Autistic Child," *Behavior Research and Therapy*, 1 (1964), 305-312.

5. R. Wahler et al., "Mothers as Behavior Therapists for Their Own Children," *Behavior Research and Therapy*, 3 (1965), 113-124.

6. R. J. Wetzel et al., "Outpatient Treatment of Autistic Behavior," *Behavior Research and Therapy*, 4 (1966), 169-177.

7. Ayllon and Michael, "The Psychiatric Nurse"; Wolf, Risley, and Mees, "Application of Operant Conditioning Procedures."

8. H. A. Murray, *Thematic Apperception Test* (New York, N.Y.: The Psychological Corporation, 1936-43).

Chapter 3

Precision Teaching:
A Useful Technology
for Special Education Teachers

Robert H. Bradfield

Reprinted by permission of the author and *Educational Technology*, August 1970

F OR QUITE SOME TIME we have seen an ever increasing array of technological devices designed to enhance the teaching process in both special and "normal" classrooms.

We have seen variation upon variation of audio-visual aids, teaching machines and computerized systems designed to expedite the transmission of knowledge from the educational system to the child. Though there is probably no question that the classroom of the future will be a computerized one in which the child's educational development will be mediated through carefully planned and constructed programed materials, at the present time there would appear to be several problems connected with such programing.

First, and possibly foremost in the minds of some, though a fiction if one thinks about it carefully, is *cost*. Our educational system is, as yet, unwilling to move to costly retooling until such time as the effectiveness of computerized programs has been proven more clearly, even though the cost over time may eventually prove to be far less if one bases the return on the amount of knowledge gained.

Second, we are still in the stage of simply storing information, at least in education. We do not have readily available computers which can make educational decisions based on the individual progress or functioning of a child. Educational programing is still in its infancy, and it must progress far beyond current levels before it can begin to approach its ultimate potential.

Finally, the range of programs which must be devised if we are to adhere to the concept of individualized instruction is so great that the problems of computerization are unquestionably multiplied. It becomes apparent that we not only have to teach children reading, writing and arithmetic, but that we are daily faced with a multitude of social behavior difficulties and needs as well. Special education provides an excellent example of such difficulties. In special programs, we face not only unique academic learning difficulties but frequently a wide range of social behavior learning requirements. We must teach Johnny to button his coat, and Mary to wash her hands. We must teach Billy to stop hitting and Kathy to stay in her seat so that learning may take place. We must teach Greg to respond differentially to sound and lip movement, and Jill to develop small-muscle skills. These and many more constitute the myriad of problems with which an advanced educational technology must cope. We now have the potential for just that kind of technology as a result of the development of the Precision Teaching method by Dr. Ogden Lindsley and others.

An adequately functioning and effective computer system requires at least two components: A language system which is consistent and which can be used and understood by all who work within the system (and hopefully by those who are outside the system) and a means of adding new information or feedback to its computation. Precision Teaching does this and much more:

- It provides a common language, a means of communication through which *all* those involved with the education of a given child may begin to communicate in precise and understandable terms.

- It requires that we become definitively precise in our description of behaviors of concern, whether they be academic, social or physical.

- It involves all aspects of the learning situation, including environmental conditions and other stimulus variables, whether these stimuli be curricular materials or social conditions, as well as the consequences which may result from behavior.

- It provides an ongoing, immediately available effect of any changes which may be attempted in order to modify the behaviors in question.

- It allows us to make precise changes in specific parts of the learning environment, either antecedent or subsequent to the behavior of concern.

- It allows us, in a very precise way, to do that which we have given lip service to for so long, to begin to "understand" the child and to let his *behavior* guide us in terms of our educational decisions.

- It provides us with a system which is not simply imposed on a child and maintained by a teacher, but a system wherein the child can very quickly take over the responsibility for his own behavior management and learning and the maintenance of all records, thereby tremendously increasing the potential applicability of such a system.

Basically, there are four components to the Precision Teaching program. The first is a system of recording and charting data in such a way that one has a continuing, readily available record of behavioral changes which may be occurring. Specific behaviors may be either accelerated or decelerated. Lindsley has developed a six-cycle logarithmic chart which, in the opinion of this writer, has a potential never before available to educators. It combines the unique qualities of precise data recording of the widest possible frequency range (frequencies ranging from one behavior every thousand minutes to one thousand behaviors every minute may be recorded on the same chart) and simplicity (though initially formidable looking, it has been dramatically shown that third graders can readily learn and chart their own behavior rates without any difficulty whatsoever).

Not only does the chart allow one to record any behavior which is definable in terms of rate of occurrence, but it has also been "calendar synchronized" in order that, whether one is carrying on one project or a thousand, a visible time representation is provided, not only from the standpoint of the daily, weekly or monthly progression of individual behaviors, but also as a comparison of beginning and ending dates of different projects.

An example of this chart is shown in *Figure 1*. Just below the abscissa, or base of the chart, the caption "Successive Calendar Days" will be noted. Just above that it will be noted that vertical lines on the chart are numbered from zero to 140. Each of these 140 lines represents one calendar day, with every seventh line (darker lines) representing a Sunday. Along the top of the chart, running horizontally, it will be noted that every fourth Sunday is marked with the numerals 4, 8, 12, 16 and 20, and above each of these numerals is a place for the day of the month and year. It can readily be seen, then, that the chart can be marked not only in terms of days of the week but in terms of weeks and months of the year in order that consistency of the time factor can be obtained in all projects in which Precision Teaching is attempted. Along the left ordinate or vertical axis of the chart, the caption "Movements per Minute" can be seen; and, just to the right of the caption, are numbers ranging from .001 to 1000. This numerical order allows one to represent visually the rate at which the specific behavior of concern is occurring. This rate is obtained by counting the frequency of occurrence of a specific behavior and dividing that frequency by the number of minutes during which counting was undertaken, hence "Movements per Minute." All data in Precision Teaching projects is graphed on a "Movements per Minute" basis. It will further be noted that from bottom to top there are six cycles on the chart, each a multiple of ten of the previous cycle. For example, .001 proceeding to .002 and so forth up to .01, at which time the count changes to .02, .03, etc. The use

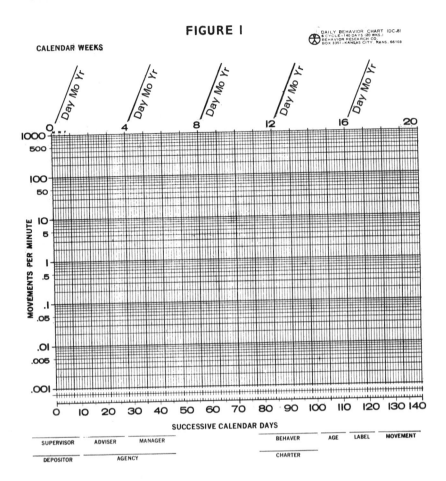

FIGURE I

of the logarithmic chart system allows a proportional representation of data, and eliminates the distortion normally obtained from "ruler" type charts.

The second component of the Precision Teaching method is the requirement of precise "pinpointing" or defining of those behaviors which one may wish to alter. It must be remembered that all data within the precision management program are based on *rate*. Lindsley has defined "pinpointing behaviors" as "movements," and he feels that an adequate pinpoint must have two basic characteristics: 1) It must have a definable beginning and end, in other words, be a complete movement cycle. For example, a "thumb sucking" movement would require that the thumb first be out of the mouth, then in the mouth, then out of the mouth in order to be a complete movement. 2) The pinpoint must pass the "dead man's test." If a dead man can do it, it can't be counted. Once behaviors of concern have been charted in this way it is possible to begin recording data in a precise and objective manner in order that we may obtain continued feedback with regard to the effect of any attempts which we might wish to make to alter that behavior.

It can therefore be seen that the two initial components of Precision Teaching involve the use of an extremely practical recording and common language system which allows both those directly involved in the project, and others as well, to quickly understand and recognize not only the purpose of the project but the progress of the individual. It brings into immediate focus both our successes and failures as teachers, and it requires that we begin to do something besides give lip service to the concept of individualized instruction. Examples of Precision Teaching projects follow.

Project Examples

One Precision Teaching project was initiated by a teacher in an attempt to decelerate the rate at which a thirteen-year-old boy tugged and pulled at her during the school day. During the week beginning Monday, October 28, 1969, this child, according to the chart kept by the teacher, was pulling and tugging at the teacher at a middle rate of four times every hundred minutes, with the rate accelerating during the week. On Monday, November 3, 1969, the teacher initiated a change in the project. She simply began turning her back on the child each time the behavior occurred. An immediate deceleration in the behavior rate began to occur. At the end of a five-week period she had successfully decelerated this behavior rate from a middle rate of four times every hundred minutes to a middle of once every hundred minutes. In other words, she decreased the behavior by a divisor of four during this five-week period.

In another project, the teacher attempted to decelerate the rate at which a boy in her program was talking out during a specific twenty minutes of the school day. Initially this talk-out rate showed approximately one talk-out per minute. In this instance, again the teacher made one simple change at the beginning of the second week, keeping all other factors constant. Each time this child talked out, she called on *another* child with his hand raised. In a six-week period, this child's talk-out rate had decreased to zero. In this case, as in all projects, there was daily, visible feedback from the chart with regard to the effect of this change on the child's behavior.

A third example is a project in which the teacher wished to decelerate the inappropriate use of the pronouns *me* and *my* and increase the use of the pronoun *I*. During the first week, or reference period, it was noted that the child inappropriately used these pronouns at a middle rate of two per minute, according to the teacher's chart. At the beginning of the second week, keeping all other variables constant, the teacher asked the child to count his own errors – and they kept a daily chart together. During the next five weeks, the child's error rate dropped from two per minute to one every two minutes. In other words, behavior frequency was divided by four. Unfortunately, this project had to be terminated at this time due to circumstances beyond the teacher's control.

Another example is that of an academic skills project designed to measure the effectiveness of a reading vocabulary building program with a young boy with a severe learning disability. In this case, the teacher felt that the child should attain a reading rate of approximately thirty words per minute on words which he had already been given before any new words were added. At the end of a three-week period, the child had attained this rate fairly consistently, and a change was initiated in which ten new words were added to his list. As expected, his rate immediately dropped to approximately ten words per minute with the addition of the new words and then gradually began to accelerate to the desired level. This is an excellent example of a curriculum project in which the teacher has allowed the *child's* behavior to determine when changes should be made in curriculum.

A final example is that of a project in which the precision charting procedure continually pointed to the *inadequacy* of the educational program, but was continually ignored. In this instance, a proficiency level of nine to ten problems per minute was indicative of readiness to proceed to a more difficult level of mathematics facts. Although there was some variation, this child, from the beginning of the project, was capable of attaining the required rate on single-digit addition facts. However, despite the evidence, the teacher continued for *six* weeks before making a change to a more difficult level. When this change was finally made (from one-digit to two-digit addition) there was *no* rate change, indicating that the child had already attained proficiency at this level. A careful examination of the child indicated that not only was he able to do addition facts at this level and much higher — he was also able to do subtraction, simple multiplication and simple division. This teacher had literally wasted everybody's time, and the child had simply learned *not* to learn for a period of almost two months. Had this teacher paid attention to her chart, this situation might have been remedied in a few days instead of months!

The IS-DOES Formula

An important component of the Precision Teaching method is the IS-DOES formula, in which Lindsley has attempted to include all of those environmental variables which might have an effect on the performance of an individual.

Not only are we far too imprecise in our designation of those variables which may affect the learning process, but even when we do attempt to become specific we too frequently mislabel these variables. Over and over again we refer to "stimuli" which do not stimulate, "rewards" which do not reward, punishment which does not punish, and so on.

If we are to fully understand learning and the uniqueness of the individuals who are part of the learning process, it is essential that we not only become more precise in identifying the components of that process, but also that we allow behavior itself to define the terms. Though we can never duplicate the rigor of a Skinnerian laboratory and maintain controls which would be ideal, we can, in the real world, at least approach such controls — if we try. The IS formula is intended to include all of the various kinds of things which exist in the individual's environment which *might* have an effect upon his behavior, while the DOES part of the formula is identical in structure except that it is composed of those events which have been identified as *having* an effect upon the pinpointed behavior.

Essentially there are five basic parts to the learning environment which are involved in the shaping or building of behavior. The IS formula is shown below.

PROGRAM/ANTECEDENT EVENT/MOVEMENT CYCLE/ARRANGEMENT/SUBSEQUENT EVENT

The PROGRAM portion of this formula includes all those things involved in the overall environmental setting, such as location, time of day, classroom seating arrangements, and so forth. An ANTECEDENT event includes all those factors which *might* result in the behavior or movement cycle and have an effect on the performance of that behavior, such as instructions, curriculum materials, demonstrations, and so forth. The MOVEMENT cycle is the behavior which is being measured, while ARRANGEMENT stands for the numerical ratio between the movement and the subsequent event. For example, one might give one M&M candy for each problem correct, in which case the arrangement would be 1:1, or one hug or statement of praise for each ten problems correct, in which case the arrangement would be 1:10. Finally, SUBSEQUENT EVENTS are those events in the environment which *may* be the result of the movement cycle, and which *may* have an effect on the future occurrence of the movement, such as praise, grades, withdrawal of privileges, smiles, and so forth.

These terms provide a much more accurate initial description of the components of the learning situation. Until we are in the position to evaluate the *effects* of these components on the behavior, it can only be said that each component has the *potential* to change behavior, but has not yet demonstrated that it will do so. Once these components have *demonstrated* a behavioral function, we then have the DOES part of the formula. It is only then that PROGRAM components can be described as DISPOSITION COMPONENTS; ANTECEDENT event components can only then be described as STIMULI; MOVEMENT CYCLES can only then be defined as RESPONSES; ARRANGEMENT components can only then be defined as CONTINGENCIES; while SUBSEQUENT EVENT components can only then be described as CONSEQUENCES. We therefore see a change from the IS formula above to the DOES formula, which follows:

DISPOSITION/STIMULUS
RESPONSE/CONTINGENCY/CONSEQUENCE

It may well be that through the development of the IS-DOES formula Lindsley has made a major contribution to education and psychology by reemphasizing the importance not only of precise behavioral definition, but also by calling attention to the fact that there are other equally important components in behavior modification procedures in addition to reinforcement. He has taken the emphasis off "M &M's" and placed it where it should be: on *the total learning process.*

The fourth and final component of the Precision Teaching system is the Behavior Bank. In this technology, as in many others, the computer has its appropriate place. The Behavior Bank is so de-. signed that those who begin to use the Precision Teaching system may "deposit" effective projects in the bank and receive in return the privilege of withdrawing other projects at a later date, thereby making the experience of people in all parts of the world directly available to any member of the bank.

For example, Miss Jones is a depositor in the bank, and she has deposited a number of successful Precision Teaching projects which are credited to her account. In the course of teaching her special class, she runs up against a problem of head banging; and, despite a series of attempts to modify this head banging, she is unsuccessful. She may then, if she so desires, contact the computer bank for help. The computer will search out projects which have demonstrated effective procedures in modifying head banging behavior, making this resource available to Miss Jones. She therefore has readily available the expertise of successful behavior modifiers with specific reference to the exact behavior with which she is concerned. At the present time, the Behavior Bank contains over six thousand behavior projects, which is only a fraction of the eventual storage potential. In this case, then, the computer is used in a highly effective manner in that it stores *successful* procedures on a multitude of problems which can be made readily available to depositors in the bank in their efforts to help children.

WE ARE LONG PAST the time when we can leave the emotional, social and academic education of children to chance. It has been pointed out far too frequently that children are over and over again exposed to a learning process which is not only painful but unproductive, at least unproductive in terms of those kinds of behaviors which we would like to build. Too frequently it is productive in terms of those very behaviors which we would like very much to get rid of. We assume learning when no learning is taking place and sadly have had no definitive ways of verifying whether or not such learning is occurring. It is high time that we begin to demand evidence that we are doing our jobs with children, not only children in general, but Johnny and Mary and Billy and Cathy. The Precision Teaching program provides at least a base for such proof and a means of evaluating what we are doing. It does not tell us what changes to make; that is left to the unique creative capabilities of each teacher. It does, however, provide that teacher with immediate feedback with regard to whether her "creativity" is resulting in a satisfactory product. As numerous writers have pointed out, failure to learn might be more appropriately called failure to teach. If we continue to avoid responsibility for assessing the effects of our teaching skills, particularly when adequate assessment techniques are available, then we are, indeed, the most immoral of practitioners.

Chapter 4

Training Parents
in Child Management *

Martha E. Bernal

T HE FLOURISHING AREA of work known as behavior modification
offers the possibility of new perceptions and roles for mental
health professionals or clinicians in child guidance as well as for
those parents and teachers who seek their services. To contrast the
new with the old roles of clinicians, I will draw upon my own experiences of thirteen years ago when I worked in an inpatient unit for
children at a psychiatric hospital.

Two of the psychologist's functions in the hospital consisted of
evaluating the personality and intelligence of referred children – using standard tests – and conducting interviews with the parents. It
was also the task of the psychologist and other professionals to un-
dertake psychotherapy with those children admitted to the unit, and
this therapy consisted of playing with the child, noting his reactions

*I am deeply indebted to the trainees and staff at the Neuropsychiatric
Institute, University of California at Los Angeles, who have worked with me
over the years, as well as to others who have assisted with the less glamor-
ous and more laborious tasks. I have been fortunate to have the invaluable
assistance of many UCLA students who have observed families over months
and years of time and suppressed their curiosity about what we were doing
with the families. Throughout the work described here, there was one person
who kept everyone – observers, trainees, and me – pointed in the right direction at the right time with the right materials at hand. Her name is Sandra J.
Sugent. Sandra also assisted in the preparation of this manuscript. This work
was partly supported by California Department of Mental Hygiene grant 2-51.

to the therapist and to the toys, and making interpretations of his behavior, very much in the manner described by V. M. Axline.[1] One purpose of the therapy was to develop a strong positive relationship with the child that could be used to influence him to change in a desirable direction. While the child was with the therapist in the play therapy room, some other professional, usually a social worker, was working with one or both parents. The social worker conducted a series of sessions during which the parents' psychological history, early family experiences, marriage, current interpersonal functioning, and relationship to their children were discussed. The aim of these discussions was to obtain a better understanding of factors contributed by the parents to the child's problems, and simultaneously to promote insight in the parents regarding their own personal difficulties in order to help them become more effective parents and interpersonal beings. Usually, play therapy sessions with the child and social casework meetings with the parents were continued indefinitely, without benefit of systematic monitoring of generalization of treatment outside the hospital, sometimes at great cost to the family in terms of time and money, and certainly at enormous cost to the public that supported the mental health agency. From the standpoint of the professional, his pattern of treatment behavior was what he had been trained to do, and he did it in the sincere belief that his treatment would benefit the family. It would take him months to form a strong positive relationship with the child, and then, at best, he would have one to three hours a week to spend with him in order to influence his behavior outside the therapy hour. From the standpoint of the parents, there frequently was the clear communication that the child had been emotionally damaged by them, and they were given no opportunity to learn how to do what the therapist was doing in order to help the child.

Having spent years of professional time in child guidance and treatment settings, I know of the protective ways manifested by professionals in these settings toward the problem child and of the blame placed upon the child's parents. Such attitudes have their expression in therapist behaviors that consist of taking the child away from his parents and closing the door to their participation in treatment. I contend that this practice has the effect of denying parents their right to become better parents, that it leaves them feeling helpless except as they continue to work with their own therapist, and gives them no effective means of helping their child other than to get him to the play therapy hour. Many facilities throughout the country offering mental health services for children continue to practice this treatment model at the present, and training centers for mental health specialists currently teach it.

Within the past decade, increasingly larger numbers of professionals who adhere to a behavior-modification model of treatment have argued that the most effective means of dealing with the child's mental health problems is to reprogram his environment so as to strengthen the behaviors he lacks and needs in order to cope adaptively, and weaken those behaviors that result in failure to cope adaptively. This reprograming is accomplished by training the important social agents in the child's environment so that they can bring about the desired change in the child. Teachers, parents, nurses, and lay volunteers, working in educational enrichment programs,[2] in regular classrooms,[3] in special classrooms for the emotionally disturbed,[4] in clinics and in the home,[5] to ameliorate behavior problems of children have been instrumental in producing beneficial changes in children. D. G. Brown describes the impact of this behavior-modification work with children for the reader who needs further convincing that it is an effective and important approach.[6]

At the basis of the behavior-modification approach is the assumption that all behavior, normal and abnormal, is learned. Abnormal behavior (such as talking "crazy" and excessive fighting), called "sick" by the traditional psychodynamic mental health establishment of the past and present, is therefore subject to the same laws of learning as normal behavior (such as reading and cooperative play). The task of the professional is to determine how to apply learning principles to teach the child to behave normally or appropriately. Once the technology for effecting the desired behavior change is developed, the role of the professional becomes one of teaching others, particularly those persons who spend the most time with the child in the settings that need to be programed or engineered. This is the changed role of the mental health professional in education and child guidance: from healer with talents and skills that are withheld from the parent, nurse, or teacher, to educator of important social agents in the child's life. Indeed, many of us see ourselves as *social educators*, teachers of skills that parents and others are not taught in the course of their own education. Such a change in the professional's role results in enhancement of the worth of social agents as people who can be relied upon to benefit the child. The change also provides hope that the enormous mental health manpower needs in this country can be met. There is already some evidence that the assumption by social agents of such therapeutic roles is more effective, efficient, and inexpensive than traditional psychotherapeutic and educational approaches to children.

My own role as educator of parents as social agents parallels that of many other workers in this area in terms of development of skills and technology for changing child and parent behavior patterns. A very incomplete list of some of these workers, all psychologists, and references to their publications, may be of interest.[7] Neither I nor most of these psychologists were trained in behavior modification during our academic education; we are "retreads," as one graduate student aptly put it. We were trained and worked as traditional psychodynamic psychotherapists, and then developed behavior-modification skills and the technology of training social agents as therapists.

During the past five years, antisocial children up to eight years of age have been the target of my efforts, and their parents have

43

taught me much about behavior modification. Since the work is based in a university hospital setting where outpatient services are provided to an immense metropolitan area, most of the parent-training techniques have been designed for teaching the parents in the clinic setting. Transfer of their newly trained skills to other settings has not been planned for in some cases, but in other cases training in the clinic has been combined with direct attempts to help the parents use their management skills in other settings via telephone consultation and/or training in those settings. My collaborators in this enterprise have been psychology pre- and postdoctoral students located at the Neuropsychiatric Institute for a year's internship in clinical psychology or training in behavior modification, and public health nurses working in the outpatient child clinic at the Institute.

THE TREATMENT PROGRAM

What is the experience of parents of an antisocial child in seeking the help of a professional doing parent training based upon learning principles? In the following pages, I hope to answer this question in terms of the way I work, starting with the initial call for help, and including a detailed account of work with the parents of a young, antisocial child. "The parent" will be referred to in the female gender, only because it is easier to do so for the sake of consistency. Whenever possible, both parents are included in training.

Details of the Target Behaviors

Two types of behavior classes need to be clarified with the parents in terms of what the child does rather than in terms of his inner experience at the time he does it. These two behavior classes are *desirable* and *undesirable* behaviors. The desirable behaviors of interest are those that parents would like to make occur more often. These behaviors could include such things as cleaning his shoes before coming into the house, doing his homework, and apologizing when he is at fault. The purpose of listing them is to provide the parents with descriptions of the child behavior that they will learn to strengthen during training. Likewise, a description and list of undesirable behaviors such as tantrums, fighting with siblings, or setting fires, provides the parents with occasions on which they will learn to behave in specified ways to discourage future occurrences of the behaviors. The parents are encouraged to recognize that the undesirable behaviors are usually disturbing to themselves and others because they occur at a high rate, are very intense, or produce serious and dangerous consequences.

Once the desirable and undesirable behaviors are identified, the parents are asked about the conditions under which these behaviors occur. Such information can provide leads regarding the stimuli anteceding the behaviors, which function to control their occurrence. Thus, the presence of a father and mother who disagree regarding the child's nap time may set the occasion for the child to tantrum and thereby produce the consequence of being allowed to skip the nap.

Consequences of the desirable and undesirable behaviors are very important; they tend to determine whether the behaviors will occur again, how frequently they will occur, and their intensity and duration. These consequences produced by the child's behavior may be social in terms of the reactions of other people to them, or tangible if some material gain or loss is involved, and may include such basic items as pain, food, warmth, etc. For example, parents may report that when the children fight, they yell at them to stop fighting. They may also say and do nothing when a child uses good manners.

Some further information about the estimated rate of occurrence of the child's behaviors and of the kinds of reinforcement schedules used is helpful. An estimate of the rate of undesirable behaviors tells the clinician how often there will be opportunities for the parents to practice their instructions. The higher the frequency of a problem behavior, the more learning trials for both child and parent. A schedule of reinforcement indicates how often or under what conditions reinforcement is being provided. For example, if a child whines every time he requests candy, and the parent tries to hold out but now and then (perhaps every third or fourth time) gives him the candy, she has reinforced the child's whining by letting it pay off intermittently. This intermittent reinforcement of the whining is one of the best schedules for maintaining behavior; in fact, it may be superior to a schedule that stipulates reinforcing each and every occurrence of the whining, since the child could become satiated on candy.

The clinician also asks questions regarding the status of the marriage, the child's history of physical illness, learning progress, and other problems, such as the presence of persons other than the immediate family in the home, and any factors complicating the current status of the family (such as financial or health hardships). However, the questions focus sharply upon behavior and behavioral interactions that occur in the present rather than upon previous history. A complete reconstruction of the previous history of the child and his family is an interesting exercise, and most likely the current problem behaviors were present or began their development during previous history. Nonetheless, the position of the behavior modifier regarding past versus present information is that reconstruction of previous history to determine the cause of a behavior disorder or deficit is time-consuming, expensive, and subject to post hoc fallacies. The crucial task is to change the child's behavior now, as soon as possible, at the least expense and hardship to his parents and others. Additional interviews may be necessary for completing the business of the first interview.

Observation and Measurement

The following are some of the behaviors that have been called antisocial: lying, tantrums, truancy from school, running away from home, theft, verbal and physical aggression toward others including peers, and noncompliance or refusal to obey. Verbal aggression is defined as name-calling, backtalk and complaining, teasing, etc., and physical aggression includes destruction of property, hitting, shoving, or other efforts to force or hurt others by physical means. If a child engages in some or all of these behaviors to a degree that is disturbing, there is a good possibility that his parents can be trained how to respond to them so that they are weakened. Before training begins, however, the frequency of occurrence of the behaviors over some unit of time (such as twenty-four hours) must be counted. Such a measurement permits monitoring of variations or changes in the target behaviors as the parent training progresses, and this monitoring of behavior frequencies is the best way available to determine whether treatment efforts are paying off.

Sometimes parents are asked to keep their own behavior records on a child,[8] while other times a trained observer is sent to the home, or to whatever setting it seems important to monitor. If the behavior problem is straightforward, as in the case of bedwetting or doing certain chores, the parents can keep a good record without having to take much time from their usual activities. In order to obtain information on some kinds of interactions between the child and parents, however, an observer must be present who is trained to reliably record them.

The home-observer or parent-observer records that are obtained prior to training are called *baseline* records. Once a baseline is obtained, the records are continued for varying periods of time after completion of a course of training during which new management behaviors have been learned. These postintervention records are compared with the baseline records to determine how much effect the training has upon the child and parents, and how durable the effects are over a period of time.

When an observer goes into a home, he is introduced to the family and then sits where he can best see everyone. He does not interact with any member of the family, and the family members are asked to ignore him and go about their usual activities but to remain in sight of the observer. Sometimes, in order to ensure that interaction will occur, the family is asked to keep the television set turned off. With clipboard and watch in hand, the observer samples periods of time for the first occurrence of each behavior in which he is interested. For example, if he is sampling every minute, he would indicate on his scoring sheet if any one of the behaviors occurs during the first minute of observation. If a behavior recurs during minute one, it is not scored again. At the end of the first minute, he goes on to minute two, scores the first occurrence of each behavior, and so on until he has scored a full session that may last from a few minutes up to several hours. This observational method, called *time sampling*, yields estimates of frequency of behavior occurrences called *time sampling scores* (TSS). To obtain approximate rates of behaviors, the TSS are expressed in terms of TSS over the length of time of an observation session.

Training Procedures

Workers in parent training have used many different devices for eliciting and strengthening appropriate parent-management behaviors, ranging from simple cueing systems to wireless radio transmitters. I use closed-circuit television to obtain live recordings of family interactions as well as for training parents. Videorecordings of the problem child with his mother and father, and at times with his siblings, permit a very close look at the current interactions that are of major interest. During the preintervention period, the family may be recorded more than once to assure a fair sample of interactions, and it may be necessary to trigger the occurrence of deviant behaviors for some children who don't show much misbehavior in the studio. To do this, the parents are given a list of things to try to get the child to do, such as bringing a magazine to the parent, leaving an intentionally planted toy or candy alone, or putting away play materials. Whether the child obeys, how soon he obeys, how he tries to disobey, what the parents say and do to try to get him to obey, how they react to his verbal or physical abuse, and any other behaviors — both parents' and child's — are important data. They are of interest because, if the child is antisocial in the ways described previously, it is certain that there is something the parents are doing that has resulted in his showing higher rates of antisocial behaviors and lower rates of desirable behaviors than other children his age living in comparable homes. The child's parents are probably failing to emit some behaviors that will strengthen and enlarge his repertoire of desirable behaviors, as well as inadvertantly reinforcing his undesirable ways. Of equal importance is the fact that, just as the parents have trained the child, the child also has trained the parents. For instance, the parents may be trained to give in to him in order to avoid his having a tantrum, or to hold him in order to prevent his wrecking other people's furniture. In short, the parents need to learn what to do instead of what they are doing. The videorecording serves as a means of capturing what they are not doing and what they need to learn to do differently.

As a training tool, the videorecordings of the parents and children are used to show where the parents are improving and what effect their new behaviors have upon the child's behaviors. In other words, videorecordings made at different points before and during training are a means of feeding back performance so that the parents know how they have changed and what remains to be changed. Sometimes various cueing devices are used. For instance, if we ask a parent to start reinforcing compliance by responding affectionately to the child contingent upon compliance, and the parent has trouble initiating her affectionate response at the right time (that is, in a contingent manner: if he complies he gets reinforced), a light can go on when the child complies that signals her to respond affectionately immediately. Later, the light can be used to signal her that she has made the right response at the right time, that is, that she has carried out the contingency of reinforcement. Sometimes, when a parent tends to oversupervise a child by constantly directing him verbally, a buzzer is activated to signal her to stop talking. These devices, and the feedback, are used because it is clear that the ways parents typically respond to their children constitute very strong habits. Since the task is to eliminate habits that lead to teaching a child to be antisocial, it is essential to use whatever techniques are necessary for training them to practice new behaviors and eliminate the old habits. Sometimes the task is to take an old habit, like affectionate praise, and rearrange its occurrence so that it is made contingent upon desirable behavior in a very deliberate way. Other times it is necessary to strengthen old but weak habits so that they occur consistently, for example, ignoring a child when he is annoying, but making sure the parent learns to ignore the annoying behavior every time it occurs.

In short, the training consists of step-by-step instructions on the use of reinforcement, punishment, and extinction, which are procedures for responding to the child that will be described later. These procedures constitute sets of behaviors that can be used when the child behaves in certain ways. The purpose of the training is to teach the parents to discriminate desirable and undesirable behaviors from the child's ongoing activity and attach new or rarely used parental behaviors to the child's activity in such a way that the consequence is to make the child improve. Each time a new set of instructions is given the parent to try out, she is provided with the opportunity to practice the instruction in direct interaction with the child while being videotaped. Then her performance is reviewed with her, with special concentration on correct performance. It is likely that such training is more effective than giving parents advice, however good the advice may be, and expecting them to change their habitual ways of responding to the child on their own. Especially when the parents and child are in the midst of an emotionally charged hassle, it would seem a very difficult task for them to react in a more effective manner unless they have had some practice with the new instructions.

CASE PRESENTATION

The following case[9] is presented to demonstrate the kinds of behavior problems manifested by a child referred to us, the ways in which his problem behaviors were being inadvertently maintained by his father and mother, how the parents were trained, the difficulties encountered in training them, and the results over time of the training. The information they gave at the first interview is summarized below.

Mitch, age two years nine months, was the only child of college-educated middle-class parents. His birth and physical and intellectual development had been normal, except that from infancy he had been highly active and they had always had difficulty getting him to obey them. In addition to hyperactivity and negativism, he was overly physically aggressive toward adults and other children, and frequently bit, kicked, and hit the children in the neighborhood with the result that their parents kept them from playing with him. Help was being sought for Mitch because the mother was seven months pregnant and the parents were fearful that Mitch would harm the new baby. They had had Mitch evaluated for the behavior problem and had been told that his prognosis for recovery was bleak since he was incapable of controlling himself. Because of this professional opinion, they were very hesitant to be firm with him.

Just before referral, another psychologist had worked with them briefly, using a reinforcement system to reward Mitch for emitting desirable behaviors. The parents had been instructed to give Mitch a small poker chip every time he did something good. The chips were transferable for candy and other goodies. Unfortunately, the system did not work well. Mitch earned handfuls of chips, which he threw back at his parents, and the chips ended up in various places around the house, including the spaghetti sauce. However, there were two valuable contributions of the treatment approach chosen by the psychologist: first, Mitch was successfully toilet trained at home by using the chips; second, the parents were already initiated into the approach. When they came for help at the suggestion of the psychologist, the mother wrote a long list of low-rate desirable and high-rate undesirable behaviors. Some of these behaviors are listed below.

Desirable

- Picks up toys.
- Washes his hands.
- Plays with his toys but only for no more than ten minutes each day.
- Puts silverware on the table.
- Watches TV quietly.
- Says "please" and "thank you."
- Goes to sleep at eight o'clock and doesn't get up during the night.
- Stays with me when we go to the department store.
- Lets my husband and me talk without interfering.

Undesirable

- Pulls clothes out of drawers and closets.
- Tantrums.
- Brings his tricycle in the house to ride.
- Puts small objects in the drain pipes.
- Makes messes around the house: writes on the walls, opens the refrigerator and takes liquid, eggs, bread, etc., and throws them all over the floor.

- Destroys property: bangs on doors and cabinets with his hands, feet, and hard objects; throws rocks, breaks dishes, climbs on furniture.
- Runs away from me in a department store or shopping center; knocks over store displays.
- Talks back, saying "shut up," "don't tell me," etc.
- When I say "no" he refuses to listen.

Some of the information regarding the conditions under which Mitch's undesirable behaviors occurred and the parents' reactions to him began to reveal their gross mismanagement of the child. Although they tended to avoid disciplining Mitch, they admitted that "when we've had it we haul off and hit him good on the behind." The spankings were given when the parents were very angry rather than in a contingent manner when the child misbehaved the first time. Following a spanking, Mitch typically would laugh and "retaliate" by engaging in another misbehavior that surpassed the previous one in degree of aversiveness. They often chased him in order to try to spank him again. To get him to bed at eight o'clock, their pediatrician had advised locking him in his room. The first night this advice was tried, he gave up crying in ten minutes and fell asleep. The next night, the parents left his door open, "hoping that he had learned his lesson." He came out of the bedroom, and they concluded that locking him in didn't work.

Mitch's destruction of property at home had been handled by removing from sight or tying down everything he could get into, and as a result the house was barren except for furniture. To keep him in the house, the parents had tied the doors with rope; they did not like to lock Mitch in or out. His aggressiveness toward others was frequently reinforced. For instance, on one of the few occasions when the mother was able to "borrow" a neighbor's child for our home-observation visit, Mitch grabbed a toy from the child and hit him on the head with it. His mother kissed him while saying it wasn't nice to hit people. Whenever he hit another child, he was never punished, but his little friend had to go along with Mitch's demands or go home. There was little mention of praising or loving the child contingent upon his occasional moments of desirable behaviors.

The next step was to begin home observation. I and Dr. W. Hansford Miller, a postdoctoral trainee working on the case with me, went to Mitch's home and subsequently sent a trained observer to begin to score the following behaviors using one-minute time sampling during weekly hour-long observation sessions:

1. Hitting and kicking and all forms of physical aggression toward others.
2. Destruction of property, including messing up, climbing on furniture, clogging drain pipes, etc.
3. Tantrums.
4. Mother commands.
5. Mitch complies.

As these baseline measurements were begun, Mitch and his parents were invited to the clinic for videorecordings on two separate occasions to make records of their interactions. Each parent was videotaped with Mitch, and the following two excerpts of the videorecordings, the first of Mitch and his mother, the second of Mitch and his father, will demonstrate some typical interactions.

Scene: The television studio was approximately fifteen by twenty feet. There were several comfortable stuffed chairs with removable seat cushions, drapes which covered a blank wall and a blackboard, a television monitor, and magazines for adults and children on a table. The parents were asked to interact with the child in whatever way they wished. The scene was very much like a waiting or reception room in an office suite. Mitch had with him a cloth tie which was used like a security blanket. His speech was somewhat unintelligible, so some minor translating was necessary.

Mother: Look at this big, big, chair, Mitchie, Mitchie.

Mitch: I don't want to sit.

Mother: You don't want to sit in this chair, Mitchie, do you want to lay down? Mitchie, I want you to sit.

Mitch: Why?

Mother: Because I expect you to. (Mitch giggles and starts running out of the room and down the hall.)

Mother: Alright Mitchie, goodbye Mitchie. (Mother runs after him.)

Mitch: Wheee! (He is being half dragged into the room and is happily swinging on his mother's arm.)

Mother: Did I tell you Daddy went to a school like this?

Mitch: Uhuh.

Mother: Daddy went here once. Do you want to get your tie, and Mommy will sit here? Go get your tie and Mommy will . . . (Mitch does not get his tie; he runs out of the room again and mother runs out after him, brings him back.)

Mother: I will tell you what, let's come over here and sit down; pick up your tie, pick up your tie Mitchie. You sit here in that nice soft chair. (Mitch doesn't pick up his tie. He runs around the room and sees the magazines and TV set.)

Mitch: Yeh — wanta color. (Mitch attempts to unlock TV cabinet.)

Mother: Mitchie, Mitchie, I don't think that they want you to do that.

Mitch: Why?

Mother: Cause I don't think they do.

Mitch: Shut up, shut up, shut up.

Mother: Okay, let's put the key away, come on, pick up your tie so that Mommy can read to you.

Mitch: Let's see television. (Mitch continues to play with the television set.)

Mother: No, No.

Mitch: Why?

Mother: Because, come on. (Mother goes to where Mitch is standing near the television, picks him up and hugs him.)

Mother: Hold Mommy tight, Mitchie, hold Mommy tight.

During these four minutes of interaction, the mother asked Mitch to pick up his tie and sit down with her a total of nine times; Mitch never obeyed. She also told him, in varying ways, to leave the TV set alone a total of five times, and he did not obey her. His noncompliance rate was zero out of fourteen commands. He also was verbally abusive by telling his mother to shut up three times, and he ran out of the room twice.

Although no instances of obedience were seen in this excerpt, the mother's high commanding rate was reinforced at other times by Mitch's very infrequent compliance to commands, or to put it in learning terms, the mother's command behavior was on an intermittent but very lean schedule of reinforcement.

She produced no aversive consequence when he failed to comply, and she positively reinforced him by swinging and holding him, being affectionate and talking to him immediately following the undesirable behaviors of running out of the room and playing with the TV set. In effect, she both allowed and reinforced noncompliance and other deviant behaviors.

The following excerpt of Mitch with his father demonstrates precisely the same interactional phenomena that were seen between Mitch and his mother.

Scene: Same as with mother. Mitch is wrecking the room by throwing all the chair pillows on the floor and draping the curtains over the big chairs.

Father: Okay.

Mitch: Yeh. (Mitch hides behind the curtain.)

Father: Did Mitchie go away?

Mitch: Shut up.

Father: Do you want to help Daddy, Mitchie? Take my jacket and put it on the chair.

Mitch: Yeh. (Mitch continues to pull down the cushions and doesn't obey while father continues to talk to him.)

Father: Do you want to help Daddy? Be Daddy's helper.

Mitch: Yeh.

Father: Why don't you pick up Daddy's jacket? Pick up Daddy's coat. Okay, Mitchie, come over here, come over here, come over here. (Father walks to Mitch and picks him up in his arms.)

> *Father:* Come on, come on, okay, Daddy's boy. Do you want
> Daddy to read to you?
>
> *Mitch:* No.
>
> *Father:* You can't do that. How about putting the pillows
> back?
>
> *Mitch:* Shut up.
>
> *Father:* Put them back, okay? (Mitch and Father are inter-
> rupted at this point.)

These patterns were more evident and pervasive in the home than in the studio. But in general these observations, together with the other information available, told us that the parents' general approach to Mitch was to pacify him at all costs. The relationship between these parents and Mitch is similar to several other parent-child combinations we have seen; it was typified as a "pacifier-blackmailer" interaction.

Training the Parents

These initial interviews and observations were completed within the first week following the parents' call, and then training began. The main task was to strengthen Mitch's compliance and desirable behaviors such as play, and weaken his severe destructiveness, tantrums, and physical aggression toward others. Since there were seven weeks of time left, it was necessary to teach the parents skills in the order in which the most rapid effect could be obtained.

Each time an instruction or intervention is described in the text below, some comments will be made regarding the use of the instructed procedure, then the instruction given the parents will be outlined briefly. Many of the comments about the instructed procedure were imparted to the parents as elaborations of the instructions as training progressed. The general approach was to get some procedure initiated (punishment, for example), give the parents training and feedback, and refine their use of it in subsequent meetings. Strong emphasis was placed on training the parents to develop a tendency to monitor their own behavior and note its effect on the child when they were with him outside the clinic. For the reader who is interested in conducting his own child-management training course based on learning principles, W. C. Becker's program for parents is very helpful,[10] as is a shorter, programed text for parents by Patterson and Gullion.[11]

Punishment: Comments. Punishment training was chosen as the first step to suppress noncompliance and other deviant behaviors because one of its characteristics is that it suppresses behavior rapidly. In varying degrees and depending upon the circumstances and ways in which it is used, it is said to have other characteristics that should be considered carefully in planning its use. Because it works rapidly and is highly reinforcing to the person doing the punishing, its effect can serve to strengthen and increase punishing rates in parents and turn them into punitive persons. A punitive parent can teach his child to be punitive and aggressive toward others by modeling; that is, the child observes the parents being successful in controlling others using aversive consequences and learns to be punitive himself. Punishment may also have various unwanted side effects such as serious emotional reactions and generation of antagonistic, retaliatory reactions in the child. Whenever punishment is used, the punishing agent should be alert to the development of these possible unwanted effects, and punishment using the application of aversive stimulation probably should be reserved for more extreme behaviors. However, it is my opinion that aversive stimulation should not be avoided under certain circumstances. It is an old-fashioned child-rearing procedure which, when properly used, has served to socialize countless numbers of well-adjusted people.

There is one general rule that is important to follow: when punishment is used, the child must be positively reinforced for good behaviors that are incompatible with the misbehaviors, and this reinforcement must occur very frequently. In this way, the child has a choice: behave acceptably and earn approval, attention and affection, or behave unacceptably and suffer aversive consequences.

Punishment involves producing reactions to the child that suppress a behavior. The reaction, called a punisher, may consist of producing an aversive consequence, such as spanking, or removing a positive reinforcer, such as putting the child alone in his room for a few minutes during which he has no social company (called *timeout*). In order for a parent to produce a punisher effectively, she must pair it with a firm warning or statement telling the child what he should do or stop doing; that is, she should specify the required behavior, and follow with the punisher if the child does not do as he is told within a brief but reasonable period of time. The parent should not wait until she has given several commands and is angry (as did Mitch's parents) before punishing, since children learn when they can afford to wait out or ignore the parents. The purpose of using a warning followed by production of the punisher is to make the warning act as a conditioned punisher. Thus, the child does not need to be punished many times before the parent can control him merely by specifying what she wants him to do. Of course, behaviors to be punished must never be reinforced, as Mitch's parents did, and, when a behavior is first put on punishment contingency (a statement that if a given behavior occurs the punisher will follow), it should be punished each time it occurs. Reactions to punishment (crying, tantrums, etc.) should be put on extinction. Instructions for this procedure are included below.

Punishment and Extinction: Instructions for Intervention I. To capitalize on the mother's accessibility for training prior to the termination of her pregnancy, she was given the opportunity to practice the instructions while the father watched in the TV control room during this and the next training sessions. The following is a summary of instructions on the use of punishment that were given to the parents:

The target behaviors for you to work on are destructiveness and physical aggression. When Mitch engages in any of these behaviors, tell him firmly to stop what he is doing, and specify his undesirable behavior. If he doesn't stop, go to where he is and spank him once on the seat. Say nothing else. If he tantrums, ignore it; act as if you are deaf, dumb and blind to its occurrence. If he runs away from you, making punishment impossible, don't chase him.

We advise parents to use spanking because it can always be produced immediately (the parent always has her hand with her), even in public places, and because it removes the problem of having to struggle with the child until they get the paddle or drag him to a timeout room. With highly aversive and young children like Mitch, I advise spanking, but check on its use at home to see that the warning rapidly takes over a controlling function and that spanking is not overused. Mitch's mother kept a record of spankings, which showed an average of ten daily spankings being administered three and four weeks after the punishment instruction. This rate seemed rather high, and we advised using timeout by putting him in his room and closing the door for a few minutes instead of relying solely on spanking. When they tried timeout, Mitch would not stay in his room, and the parents reluctantly agreed to put a lock on the door.

Extinction: Comments. Ignoring Mitch's tantrums is called extinction, and involves responding to the child with neither reinforcer or punisher; to put it simply, the child gets no attention of any kind as long as he engages in annoying behavior. Extinction is a means of weakening behaviors that are neither dangerous nor destructive, but mostly bothersome or inappropriate. Because annoying behavior is bothersome, others frequently attempt to suppress it by criticizing and correcting the child. Although such reactions are negative, they most likely serve as reinforcers since the intent of the child often is to annoy others. As in the use of punishment, ignoring must be immediate and consistent, and behaviors on extinction should never be reinforced or punished. When a behavior is first put on extinction, it is useful to tell the child that the parent will attend to him when he stops emitting the annoying behavior, and the child should have the behavior described or specified to him so that he knows what to stop doing in order to earn back the parents' attention.

Reinforcement: Comments. The parents were instructed on the use of positive reinforcement during the second training session. It was considered very important to have the parents reinforce Mitch for desirable behaviors to offset the aversiveness of punishment, and to provide the child with a means of earning positive reactions.

Reinforcement involves producing a reaction to the child that strengthens a behavior. The reaction is very much like rewarding the child with something he likes, or that is pleasurable. In learning or behavior-modification language, the reward is called a reinforcer, and may consist of producing a pleasant consequence, such as affection or a piece of candy, or removing a punisher, or giving back the privilege of watching television when that privilege has been previously taken away. To use reinforcement effectively, the reinforcer must be produced immediately following the desirable behavior, and the punisher must be removed immediately. In training parents, I have relied most heavily on production of reinforcers rather than removal of punishers because this procedure is more straightforward and less confusing to the novice. I also prefer to rely on social reinforcers such as parental affection, praise, approval, and other positive forms of attention (if these reinforcers result in strengthening of the desirable behaviors) rather than upon tangible reinforcers such as tokens, candy, money, and toys. Tangible reinforcement systems have been shown to produce significant improvement in children, but they also tend to require more planning and care on the part of the parents, and sometimes can end up in much confusion and haggling between parent and child. There are presently no data to show that children whose parents primarily use social reinforcers are any better or worse off than children whose parents emphasize use of tangible reinforcers. Most children will respond to both. There are ways to use tangible reinforcers effectively, and for this information the reader is referred again to Patterson and Gullion,[12] and Becker.[13] When the parents are capable of being affectionate toward their child, and the child seeks their attention and approval, I try to get them to program their social reinforcers so as to make them occur contingent upon desirable behaviors. I have also advised allowing a child to engage in some behavior that has a high frequency in his repertoire (that he likes to do and spends a lot of time doing) as a reinforcer for some low-rate behavior that the parent wants to strengthen.[14] This use of "activity" reinforcers is called the Premack principle, and has been applied successfully to many other problems by others.[15]

Reinforcement: Instructions for Intervention 2. The instructions given Mitch's parents were as follows:

Whenever Mitch is playing appropriately with a toy or object, reinforce him by immediately attending to him, praising, talking to him, and acting affectionately. Tell him what he is doing that pleases you.

Practice of Punishment, Extinction, and Reinforcement: Intervention 3. The third intervention occurred on the fourth week after the second intervention; three weeks of time were lost because our television equipment was stolen. Also, at the time of this intervention the mother was one week from fullterm and did not feel well enough to come to the clinic. Therefore, the session was used to review and refine the father's use of punishment, reinforcement, and extinction, and to have him list and look for instances of desirable behaviors to reinforce. It was stressed that he especially reinforce compliance and behaviors that were competing with undesirable behaviors (such as Mitch riding his tricycle outside instead of inside the house).

Practice of Reinforcement: Intervention 4. The baby, a girl, was born as scheduled on the eighth week following the initial interview with the parents. Two weeks later, the father returned to the studio for additional practice, particularly on reinforcement of different kinds of desirable behaviors. This additional practice was necessary because Mitch's parents, along with other parents we have seen, tended to expect desirable behaviors and to neglect reinforcing them.

Consistency: Instructions for Intervention 5. During the week following Intervention 4, the observer reported inconsistency between the parents in their management of Mitch. Both parents were invited to participate in Intervention 5, which was designed to emphasize consistent reactions to Mitch by both parents. The following instructions were given to them:

> Essentially you can best work together by supporting or backing each other up. For example, if father asks Mitch to pick up his crayons, or to stop running around, then mother can support him by not allowing Mitch to get her positive attention until he has obeyed. If she has to attend, then she can respond in terms of the father's command, for example, "Mitch, pick up the crayons as your father asked."
>
> When you punish for misbehavior, it is very important that you both be consistent. When one of you punishes Mitch, the other must not reward him with attention until he is acceptable again. Also, follow up your commands immediately with a punisher so that you don't have to repeat them over and over.
>
> It is important that you support each other when possible concerning his acceptable behavior. In other words, show Mitch that it pleases you both when he is acceptable with both of you present. When Mitch sees that you both work together in rewarding him and setting limits, he will find it easier to do as you wish.

One week later, the mother called to report that Mitch was very jealous of his sister. When asked to describe what she saw him do that caused her to assume he was jealous, she said that he had begun to engage in many of his destructive behaviors during the time she was feeding, changing, or otherwise caring for the baby. When this happened, she put the baby down and went after Mitch to try to punish him. He also had insisted on sleeping with his parents, and they had allowed it but did not wish to continue this practice.

Insofar as was possible, such problems were handled by urging the mother to work out her own solutions. She was asked what she could do about the difficulties, in terms of what she had been taught. She was given approval for correct answers and help in thinking of ways in which Mitch could get her positive attention other than by being deviant. The mother decided to ignore Mitch's deviant behavior during care of the baby, but to have him help her do various things for the baby, such as preparing the bottle, and to reinforce him for desirable behavior occurring in the stimulus situation of caring for the baby. She was advised to put Mitch to bed affectionately, but to ignore any tantrums and lock his door if necessary. These decisions were carried out by the parents according to their report, but there were no data to monitor their direct effects.

Reading and Discussion of Living with Children: Intervention 6. When Patterson and Gullion's *Living with Children*[16] became available to us, the parents were supplied with a copy and we met with them to discuss the book. Each had independently and successfully responded to questions we asked in order to determine their knowledge of the learning principles and management techniques described in the book. As a result of reading the book, they recognized some mistakes in managing Mitch that they had not noticed previously. One example given by the mother was Mitch's running away from her when she was trying to punish him by using timeout. Chasing after him merely made it a game for Mitch, and he was being reinforced for running away. Instead, she said she realized that she should punish only if it could be effectively administered, and that any attempts by Mitch to taunt her into chasing him (for example, he would stand outside a window with a brick in hand and call to her) should be ignored. The book also convinced them that they should get an effective lock put on his door (this was our first inkling that several locks had failed to keep Mitch in his room) and that timeout was, after all, a useful procedure. A good part of the discussion during this intervention was used to point up the importance of teaching Mitch to discriminate those circumstances (time and place) in which he could engage in certain behaviors and those in which the same behavior was forbidden. This discussion arose with regard to Mitch's use of the water hose on the living room carpet. Use of reinforcement for using the hose properly while watering the lawn under his father's supervision and punishment or no reinforcement for using it improperly were suggested, and the parents readily understood the rationale for the suggestion. Following this discussion, the parents were urged to contact Dr. Miller or myself should problems arise in the future.

Treatment Effects

Figures 1, 2, and *3* provide a weekly report of the observer's measurements in Mitch's home up to the 22nd week. There were two followups: one at 33 weeks and another at 60 weeks. Each followup consisted of two hourly observations on consecutive days, and the data points shown on the graph are averages for the two days. Along the bottom of each graph are plotted weeks of time and points where the six interventions took place. Week 1 was the week during which baseline measurements were made. The mother's health prevented observations at points designated as "missing data." Along the side of the graph are plotted the actual TSS occurring within each 60-minute observation. A maximum score of 60 was possible for any one observation session.

In *Figure 1* and *Figure 2,* effects of the first intervention, designed to reduce hitting and kicking, destructiveness, and tantrums were seen immediately by comparing the baseline measurement with the data point for week 2, when the mother was instructed on punishment and extinction of these behaviors. The sharply reduced rate of these three behaviors during subsequent weeks was followed by an apparent increase in destructiveness and tantrums at week 7, just before Mitch's sister was born. The home observer reported, however, that the increase was only quantitative, and that Mitch's destructiveness and tantrums had actually diminished in intensity and duration. For example, where he had once kicked a chair violently across the room, he now gently laid it on its side. Followup at 33 and 60 weeks showed unusually good durability of intervention effects.

Figure 3 shows the degree to which Mitch complied with his parents' commands and requests. The compliance measure was derived by dividing the TSS of commands given him by both parents into the number of commands Mitch obeyed within the same minute in which the command was given. The result was multiplied by 100 to produce percent compliance. Compliance of 100 percent meant that Mitch obeyed every command given him. The baseline point at week 1 shows only 3 percent compliance, and as soon as Intervention 1 took place, the child's compliance increased to 50 percent. There was some evidence that the parents were using the punishment instructions given them for control of destructiveness and hitting to obtain compliance from Mitch, thus accounting for this rapid and large effect. At week 3, positive reinforcement for compliance was actually begun. By the week before the birth of his sister, Mitch was obeying nine out of ten commands. In subsequent weeks, he maintained his compliance above the baseline score, albeit there were some fluctuations. Followups at weeks 33 and 60 showed that a gradual drop in compliance had occurred, from 100 percent at week 22 to 64 percent at week 60.

To summarize, the instructions had immediate and powerful effects upon the child's target behaviors. At followup fourteen months later, all behaviors still showed considerable improvement over baseline, but the increase in destructiveness and drop in percent compliance suggested possible problems for the future that would have to be checked as time went on.

The followup at 60 weeks took place exactly a year after the baby's birth, and the parents reported that their worst fears had not been realized. Mitch had never harmed his sister and was very protective of her. On the negative side, the home observers noted that on various occasions the mother still was not applying some of the learning principles and procedures that we had taught her. As an example, the mother herself reported that, when she was present, Mitch cried or ran away rather than hit back when another child hit him. It was suggested that she think of teaching Mitch to discriminate those occasions when he could hit back (for example, when he was hit first by another boy his size) and those occasions when he could not hit back (for example, when he was hit first by a girl, or by a younger child). She was urged to help Mitch assert himself verbally

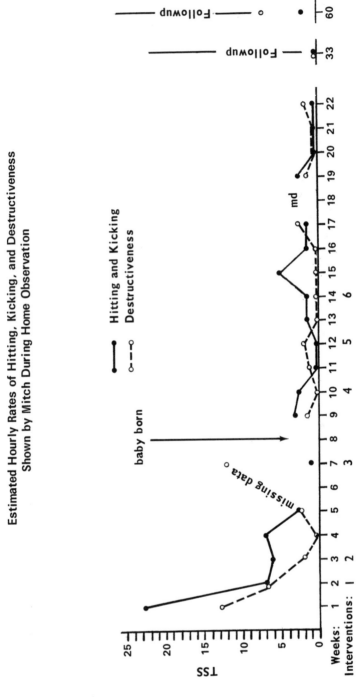

FIGURE 1

Estimated Hourly Rates of Hitting, Kicking, and Destructiveness
Shown by Mitch During Home Observation

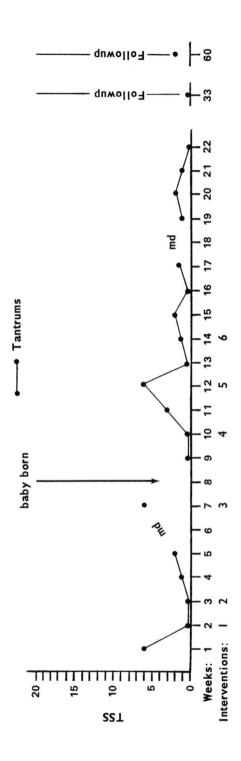

FIGURE 2
Estimated Hourly Rates of Tantrums
Shown by Mitch During Home Observation

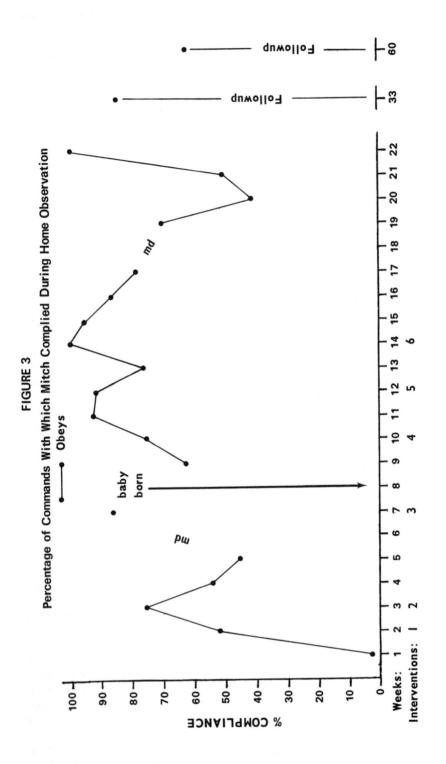

FIGURE 3

Percentage of Commands With Which Mitch Complied During Home Observation

with the other child and to have him warn the other child of impending punishment if he was hit again. It was also suggested that she help Mitch by prompting him on what to say and praising his appropriate use of assertive speech. Another example of mismanagement was the mother's occasional reinforcement of deviant behavior by holding Mitch tenderly to stop his ongoing activity.

From the foregoing observations at followup, it appeared that the parents would need periodic consultation regarding their handling of Mitch. They again were assured of its availability and invited to read a copy of Becker's book.[17] The mother was most grateful for the continued monitoring of Mitch's progress and expressed relief that consultation would be available.

DISCUSSION

Mitch and his parents represent one of our most successful attempts at parent training of antisocial children. Success and failure are never clearcut, and there are varying degrees of change in rates of deviant behaviors relative to baseline measurements. Using the format for intervention that has been described, along with consultation via telephone, we have found significant and durable improvement (from one to three years after the initial interview) in three boys and one girl who had varying types and degrees of noncompliant, negativistic, and aggressive behaviors but who were otherwise normal.[18] In these four cases, up to seven parent-training sessions in the television studio were required. With two other five-year-old boys who were matched on the basis of a number of variables,[19] it was difficult to evaluate improvement because the behaviors of the children in the studio varied greatly and did not provide sufficient opportunities for the parents to practice instructions and because of unreliable parental record-keeping. The mother of a sixth child demonstrated her ability to manage him more effectively on occasion but she ended up in a psychiatric hospital and there were no followup data.[20] We are currently working with a five-year-old seventh child whose mother is constantly supervising him despite repeated attempts to teach her to reduce verbal supervision and increase use of positive reinforcement using our standard training with television feedback in the studio as well as training at home.[21]

The mothers of the sixth and seventh children have taught us that social education of parents in child management is the easier of two aspects of work with parents of antisocial children. When education is insufficient to produce the desired change, a much more difficult aspect of the work is the engineering of environments in which parents live in order to bring about change in their child management behaviors. This work is difficult because there is meager knowledge about how to do it, and because, as professionals, we usually have limited access to the reinforcers in the parents' lives. For instance, the divorced mother of the sixth child, a boy, did not adhere to any routine schedules of housekeeping or child rearing.

Having been unable to keep jobs because of her irregularity and interpersonal problems, she obtained the psychiatric verification necessary to place herself on the psychiatrically disabled list in California so she could be supported by the state. As the state-allowed period of her psychiatric disability approached its end, she began to increase the frequency of her inappropriate behaviors and pleaded with the clinician to hospitalize her and the boy. Since, in the opinion of various professionals, neither she nor the boy were judged to be in need of hospitalization, her plea was denied. She was also denied psychiatric verification for a second period of disability payments. Instead, she was offered a carefully conceived program designed to get her back on the way to being able to obtain and hold a job and to strengthen her routine housekeeping behaviors. Following the beginning of this program, she left the city with the boy and many attempts were made to induce her to come back; among these attempts was a trip to see her. She made and then broke a promise to return to Los Angeles, and we received word that she had tried to get herself admitted to another hospital but had been told to come back to us if she wanted treatment. Subsequently, following a second attempt at suicide using the boy's medication for behavior disorder, she was admitted to a hospital. There is no information as yet regarding the boy's whereabouts. This case emphasized the challenges presented by some parents. Often we wondered if the boy would be better off with a foster family (she was willing to give him up), but realized that foster families were hard to find, and there was no guarantee of a more beneficial environment for the child. Had we controlled the money the mother needed in order to subsist, it might have been possible to use it as a reinforcer to teach her new ways of dealing with her environment. As it was, the social system offered her the payoff of compensation for behaving in a deviant manner, and gave her total care for being sufficiently deviant.

In the case of the seventh child, his mother hovers over him constantly to prevent any misbehavior before he ever engages in it. This practice has the effect of making the child retaliatory and teaching him to be punitive toward others. Since no amount of training has reduced her supervisory activity sufficiently, we are trying a different tack. She has permitted the placement of a package for monitoring interactions in her home because she cares for the child and wants to do whatever is necessary to help him. The package contains a cassette recorder which is controlled by a timer that turns on the recorder four times during the day sometime between 7:00 AM and 8:00 PM and provides about thirty minutes' daily recording. Once the timer is set for periods when the children are all at home, the package is locked. The cassette cartridge is changed daily by an assistant. The mother knows that recordings are being made, but not the exact time, and understands that if there is a possibility that something has been recorded that she does not want us to hear, she may keep the tape. A baseline of her verbal commanding and reinforcing behaviors is currently being obtained. Her rate of verbal commanding obtained via home recorder already promises to be considerably higher than her current mean rate of 88 per hour obtained by the home observer. (This rate is 100 less than the baseline obtained before training in the studio began 30 weeks ago.) That is, her commanding and reinforcing rates as she is being monitored by the clinician in the TV studio and observer in the home seem to be inconsistent with her performance when she does not know when she is being monitored.

If the training produces change in the parent's management behaviors, but she reverts back to old habits when degree of monitoring is at a minimum (maximum monitoring would be observation in the studio during videorecording), then some other methods need to be invented to engineer generalization of her improvement to situations in which she is not being monitored. The experimental approach of the behavior modifier is the backbone and foundation upon which he can rely to solve such problems. With a means of monitoring in the home without the presence of an observer already available, we can use the obtained rates of supervising and reinforcing as baserates against which some possible solutions to the engineering problem can be tested. One solution may be to program or instruct the boy to reinforce his mother's pleasant and affectionate behavior toward him. The outcome of this solution could be that the mother's reinforcing behaviors would rise above baseline rates, and that, by virtue of the increased pleasantness between them, the mother's reinforcing could be maintained indefinitely.

The problem of excessive supervision is another matter, however. Since the boy complies now and then, she gets reinforced for supervising, and the occasional reinforcement keeps her supervisory rate high. In addition, she gets reinforced by her two other children for supervising, and the overall amount of reinforcement may be very high. A possible solution could be to try to program all three children to react in some way to her that would reduce supervision, but one of the children is not old enough to follow instructions although he gets his share of supervision.

After testing the effects of programing the boy (and perhaps his 8-year-old sister as well) to reinforce his mother's pleasant reactions, if no lasting changes are produced, we may try evaluating the effects of paying the mother amounts of money for reducing supervision and increasing reinforcement above the baserates. Following a period of time using money as a reinforcer, the money can be withdrawn and the durability of its effects evaluated.

Such is the young state, in one laboratory, of the art and science of parent training. Patterson has developed more elaborate and innovative social engineering programs for intervening in families of deviant children. [22] The future development of technology for social education and engineering promises to be an exciting experience. It is destined to have profound effects upon the roles and practices of people providing human services as well as upon some of our social ills that are badly in need of intervention.

NOTES

1. V. M. Axline, *Play Therapy,* rev. ed. (New York, N.Y.: Ballantine Books, 1969).

2. R. Ulrich, M. Wolfe, and M. Bluhm, "Operant Conditioning in the Public Schools," *Educational Technology Monographs,* 1 (1968), No. 1; M. W. Hill, R. H. Mattson, and N. K. Buckley, "Special Class Placement as a Treatment Alternative for Deviant Behavior in Children," *Modifying Deviant Social Behaviors in Various Classroom Settings,* ed. F. A. M. Benson (Eugene, Ore.: University of Oregon, 1969), No. 1.

3. W. C. Becker et al., "The Contingent Use of Teacher Attention and Praise in Reducing Classroom Behavior Problems," *Journal of Special Education,* 1 (1967), 287-307; L. Homme, *How to Use Contingency Contracting in the Classroom* (Champaign, Ill.: Research Press, 1969).

4. F. Hewett, "Educational Engineering with Emotionally Disturbed Children," *Exceptional Children,* 33 (1967), 459-467.

5. R. Wolf, T. Risley, and T. Mees, "Application of Operant Conditioning Procedures to the Behavior Problems of the Autistic Child," *Behavior Research and Therapy,* 1 (1964), 305-312; R. G. Wahler and M. Erickson, "Child Behavior Therapy: A Community Program in Appalachia," *Behavior Research and Therapy,* 1 (1969), 71-78.

6. D. G. Brown, "Behavior Modification with Children," *Children,* (in press).

7. C. D. Williams, "The Elimination of Tantrum Behavior by Extinction Procedures," *Journal of Abnormal and Social Psychology,* 59 (1959), 269; R. G. Whaler et al., "Mothers as Behavior Therapists for Their Own Children," *Behavior Research and Therapy,* 3 (1965), 113-124; R. P. Hawkins et al., "Behavior Therapy in the Home: Amelioration of Problem Parent-Child Relations with the Parent in the Therapeutic Role," *Journal of Experimental Child Psychology,* 4 (1966), 99-107; K. D. O'Leary, S. O'Leary, and W. C. Becker, "Modification of a Deviant Sibling Interaction Pattern in the Home," *Behavior Research and Therapy,* 5 (1967), 113-120; G. R. Patterson, R. S. Ray, and D. A. Shaw, "Direct Intervention in Families of Deviant Children," *Oregon Research Institute Research Bulletin,* 8 (1968), No. 9; G. R. Patterson, D. A. Shaw, and M. J. Ebner, "Teachers, Peers, and Parents as Agents of Change in the Classroom," *Modifying Deviant Social Behaviors in Various Classroom Settings,* ed. F. A. M. Benson (Eugene, Oreg.: University of Oregon, 1969), No. 1; R. G. Tharp and R. J. Wetzel, *Behavior Modification in the Natural Environment* (New York, N.Y.: Academic Press, 1969).

8. G. R. Patterson and M. E. Gullion, *Living with Children: New Methods for Parents and Teachers* (Champaign, Ill.: Research Press, 1968); O. R. Lindsley, "An Experiment with Parents Handling Behavior at Home," *Johnstone Bulletin,* 9 (1966), 27-36.

9. W. H. Miller, "Training Parents in the Management of a Hyperaggressive Child." Paper presented in symposium: *Some Factors in Planning Child Management Training for Parents of Outpatient Children,* at the meetings of the California State Psychological Association, Monterey, California, 1970.

10. W. C. Becker, *Teaching Children. A Child Management Program for Parents* (Champaign, Ill.: Englemann-Becker Corporation, 1969).

11. Patterson and Gullion, *Living with Children.*

12. Ibid.

13. Becker, *Teaching Children.*

14. M. E. Bernal, "Training a Mother to Strengthen Solid Food Eating in Her Child." Unpublished manuscript, 1970.

15. Homme, *How to Use Contingency Contracting in the Classroom.*

16. Patterson and Gullion, *Living with Children.*

17. Becker, *Teaching Children.*

18. M. E. Bernal et al., "Behavior Modification and the Brat Syndrome," *Journal of Consulting and Clinical Psychology,* 32 (1968), 447-455; M. E. Bernal, "Behavioral Feedback in the Modification of Brat Behaviors," *Journal of Nervous and Mental Diseases,* 148 (1969), 375-385; M. E. Bernal, "Training a Mother."

19. M. E. Bernal, S. Young, and G. Shannon, "Application of a Procedure for Modification of Brat Behaviors." Unpublished manuscript, 1969.

20. P. A. Reagor, "The Case of Bill and Mrs. C." Paper presented in symposium: *Some Factors in Planning Child Management Training for Parents of Outpatient Children,* at the meetings of the California State Psychological Association, Monterey, California, 1970.

21. D. E. Williams, "Training of an Educationally Limited and Indigent Mother in Child Management." Paper presented in symposium: *Some Factors in Planning Child Management Training for Parents of Outpatient Children,* at the meetings of the California State Psychological Association, Monterey, California, 1970.

22. Patterson, Ray, and Shaw, "Direct Intervention in Families of Deviant Children."

II

Methods:

BEHAVIOR MODIFICATION

AND THE REMEDIATION OF LEARNING DISABILITIES

THE ARTICLES in this section focus upon the three most frequently encountered difficulties of learning-disabled children: reading, language, and maintenance of attention.

Gray presents a programed conditioning technique designed to increase the reading skills of a wide variety of children with reading problems. This program is currently undergoing extensive research, and to date the results suggest that this unique and innovative approach may provide us with an extremely valuable procedure in our attempts to remediate reading disabilities.

In Chapter 2, Stark presents first a brief discussion of language development in both normal and atypical children, and he discusses the major types of difficulties that appear in the language-impaired child. Following this, a system of clinical management is presented that utilizes programed learning procedures, and Stark provides a carefully detailed example of a step-by-step procedure that can be effective in helping such children.

The final chapter of this section, by Martin and Powers, focuses upon one of the most misunderstood aspects of learning disabilities. Since the time of Strauss and his followers, the presumed neurological bases of the short attention spans of many learning-disabled children has tended to suggest an irreversibility, or at least poor prognosis, for change. The authors attempt to dispel such assumptions, and they provide a strong case for the recognition of attention span as an operant behavior that is learned and therefore modifiable through operant techniques.

Chapter 1

A Behavioral Strategy
for Reading Training

Burl B. Gray

A TREMENDOUS volume of literature has been published on how to teach reading and remedial reading, and it presents an incredible variation of hypotheses, materials, and techniques. For the most part, these various methods stress the importance of specific materials or teaching techniques. Very few are systematically aimed at the student's learning performance. Despite the findings of studies that indicate that the principles of learning are central to the acquisition of reading skill,[1] many procedures appear to attend to everything but direct work on the skill acquisition of the target performance, that is, the act of reading. Some people apparently feel more comfortable working with hypothetically generated peripheral antecedents to the reading failure.

S. A. Cohen has aptly suggested that there seems to be confusion on the part of some people between teaching and learning.[2] Children who fill our remedial-reading classes have failed to learn to read, but they have had plenty of *teaching*. Teaching that does not result in learning is nonfunctional and is a waste. The teacher who says, "I taught him but he failed to learn," did not teach, and therefore is a failure as a teacher.

Overt attention to, and use of, learning principles in reading, while not common in education, nevertheless is not new. The efficacy of a behavioral strategy in reading training has been well established.[3] As a form of reemphasis of these results, there is a growing awareness that the critical issue is to teach the child to break the printed language code — do it thoroughly and do it quickly.[4]

The plan for this article, then, is to present a behavioral approach to training in reading. The strategy is one which responds to three basic points: (1) teaching the code, (2) performance of the child, and (3) teacher activity. The approach is very pragmatically behavioral. Thus, the rationale responds to the realities of the presenting environment rather than to the historical precedent in the literature on reading.

Rationale

Many definitions of reading ability include both a decoding skill and a comprehension ability. It is extremely difficult to comprehend a message that you cannot decode. Therefore, the first priority should be to teach the decoding skill. Thus, our approach is concerned with teaching the child to break the printed language code.

Since it is desirable to teach this as quickly and effectively as possible, the techniques of instructional programing are used. That is, the instructional plan is organized in a logical, sequential order. Within this order, the magnitude of difference between contigious steps should be adjusted so that a child can, with a defined level of success, move through the various steps (which are called *difficulty levels*). This tends to minimize two undesirable situations. One is the situation in which the student is retained in each difficulty level for a period of time greater than is necessary for his mastery of that level. The other situation occurs when the student is accelerated too rapidly through difficulty levels so that he does not achieve mastery of each level as he proceeds.

The most straightforward method of determining the balance between efficient acceleration and inappropriate acceleration is to monitor the student's performance in terms of successful (or correct) responses. The proportion of correct responses that a student generates is, in part, determined by the rate at which he is being accelerated through difficulty levels. When movement through difficulty levels exceeds ability, correct responding decreases. When movement through difficulty levels is exceeded by ability, correct responding becomes excessively high. Thus, the level of correct responding by the student can be controlled by changing the difficulty of the performance task.

The student's performance also is influenced by another important aspect of the situation, which is the teacher's management of reinforcers and punishers contingent upon each response. The frequency of any given response can be increased and the variability of responses to a given stimuli can be reduced by making a reinforcer contingent upon those responses. Conversely, the frequency of a particular response can be reduced and the variability of responses to a given stimuli can be increased by making a punishment contingent upon those responses. The teacher, then, can exercise a considerable amount of influence over the level of correct responding of the student by controlling both the acceleration rate through difficulty levels of task performance and the consequences that are made contingent upon correct and error responses.

Our reading program (Monterey Institute for Speech and Hearing, California) places major emphasis upon these parameters of acceleration rate and reinforcement as a means of obtaining the necessary performance levels from the student. A detailed discussion of the management of these parameters will be presented later in this article.

Procedure

The reading-training procedure is called Performance Determined Instruction (PDI). A previous publication has described the architecture of this system.[5] To provide continuity for the present discussion, a description of PDI adapted from that article will be presented here.*

Performance Determined Instruction — Reading

In designing the system, we have made various assumptions. These are based upon empirical data and principles of learning. The four major premises of PDI are:

- Reading is a learning task; therefore, it is responsive to the laws of learning.
- Decoding is antecedent to comprehension; therefore, it should be attended to first.
- The system should provide success in abundant quantities and should provide frequent and immediate reward for that success.
- Characteristics such as visual perception, IQ, visual-motor coordination, and visual and auditory sequencing are considered not to differentially affect prognosis for skill mastery unless the deficiency is of such a marked and gross degree that it results in reduced functional ability in nonreading activities.

Training Procedure

All children who come to the clinic are initially evaluated in terms of their current level of performance in reading. Following this evaluation, the child is assigned to the PDI reading-training procedure if he has demonstrated at least a minimum level of performance ability. This mimimum criteria for inclusion in PDI requires that he must have knowledge of the alphabet and the most common sound-symbol relationships. If the child does not demonstrate mastery at this minimum level during the evaluation session, he is placed in an alternate program, which is a prereading-training situation. This procedure is based upon branching programing techniques.[6] The routine

*The author gratefully acknowledges the assistance and contributions of Mr. Richard Baker and Miss Susan Stancyk in the development and clinical application of PDI.

of this pretraining activity is simple and straightforward; it is common in the psychological literature on task mastery. Only children who demonstrate a lack of skill in this area are placed in this activity.

Once a child has been placed in PDI, he is grouped with one other child of approximately similar abilities. Thus, each training session involves one teacher and two students. Training sessions are thirty minutes to one hour long and are held one to five times a week. Precise schedule determination is based upon the intersect strategy, which will be discussed later.

The thirty-minute training sessions in PDI are divided into two performance activities. The first fifteen minutes of a training session are devoted to training in word-attack skills. Specifically, this involves the reading of words on a word list. The lists of words increase in difficulty in a sequential manner in terms of phonetic complexity and word length.

The beginning word lists are composed of CVC words (consonant-vowel-consonant words, not nonsense syllables) in which the vowel is held constant throughout the entire difficulty level. A new target vowel signals a new difficulty level. The word lists progress from this form in the beginning until all short vowels have been introduced. The word lists then increase in complexity by the sequential introduction of longer words, consonantal clusters, blends, and polysyllabic words.

One of the two students will begin reading his word list aloud. The teacher, who keeps a record of correct, correct-reinforced, and error responses on a tally sheet, dispenses poker-chip tokens for correct performance (correct reading of a word) according to the particular reinforcement schedule in effect at that time. When one child makes an error, the other child is then given an opportunity to perform on his word lists. Error responses may be pointed out by the teacher, but there is no emphasis on error responses nor any practicing of error responses. An error response is simply an event that has occurred and that is not counted as correct or rewarded, and it is not counted towards the accumulation of a reward. The occurrence of an error response causes the transfer (from one student to the other) of the opportunity to read. The teacher is the sole judge of the correctness of a response. This procedure is continued until the first fifteen minutes of the session have elapsed.

During the second fifteen minutes, the activity switches to contextual reading. Each student, based upon the initial evaluation, is placed in a graded reading series at a starting point below his tested reading grade level. During the second fifteen-minute segment, one student will read from his graded reading-series book. For each correct sentence he receives one poker-chip token. When he makes an error response, the second child is given the opportunity to read from his reader. Again, the teacher activity is one of keeping a record of correct, correct-reinforced, and error responses. In addition, the teacher dispenses the poker chips and manages the transfer of response opportunity during the session.

If a child continues to respond correctly for three minutes during either the first or second fifteen-minute segment of a training session, he is stopped by the teacher. At that point the teacher gives him a bonus chip and transfers response opportunity to the second student. This is done so that each student will have more than one opportunity to perform during each segment of a session. At the end of each daily session, the poker chips are redeemable for M&M's at a conversion rate of five chips for each M&M. During the time when one student is responding, the other student merely sits quietly and awaits his turn. This situation is consistent during all training activities. For one-hour sessions, the thirty-minute cycle is merely repeated.

Materials

In PDI activities the main emphasis is upon teacher activity rather than upon particular materials per se. Consequently, a wide latitude is permitted in the choice of materials. The general guideline is that word-attack material (word lists) should be presented in such a manner that the introduction of target phonemes is controlled and sequential. This usually means that difficulty and complexity increases in some type of linear manner throughout the course of the material. In the present instance, material was taken from L. Bloomfield or R. Flesch.[7] Later explanation of the PDI system will relate specifically to the Flesch word lists.

In the contextual (sentence) reading area, materials such as graded reading texts are used.* Again, wide latitude is permitted in the selection of the materials, the basic requirement being that the material be presented in some type of sequentially graded manner. Among the variety of graded texts that are available, the choice is often dictated by the student's topic interest level. There is no necessary correlation between the words on the word-list material and the words in the sentence-reading material.

Training Management

Decision making is often related to an intuitive process called *clinical judgment,* or *teacher judgment,* or *clinical inference.* Today there is a sufficient body of evidence to conclude that (a) the amount of professional training and experience of the judge does not relate to his judgmental accuracy, and (b) the validity of the judgment is not related to the amount of information available to the judge.[8] Thus, intuitive judgment is not reliable nor necessarily valid. In addition, L. R. Goldberg states that "...rather simple actuarial formulae typically can be constructed to perform at a level of validity no lower than that of the clinical expert."[9]

---

*In the PDI program, graded reading texts are utilized from a number of sources, among which are texts published by Heath Publishing Co., Harper & Row, Harr and Wagner Co., and Behavioral Research Laboratories.

Since the main object of the PDI system is to provide an efficient means of high-precision learning of a decoding skill, some requirement of performance levels (performance targets) has to be established. Also, procedures have to be developed to cause the performance of the child to approximate the target. Then, some method of decision making has to be arrived at in order to determine which of the various procedures will be employed and when they will be employed.

Therefore, in an effort to provide a standardized type of training management and to provide a uniformally valid process for making such decisions, a model was constructed following the Test-Operate-Test-Exit (TOTE) procedures used in some forms of computer logic. The specific fundamentals selected for the design of the present model were taken from G. A. Miller, E. Galanter, and K. H. Pribram.[10]

Based upon preliminary work at the Institute in 1968, it was decided that performance limits would be set for the performance of the word-list activity only.[11] The target performance was 92 percent correct responding. The target range was ± 2 percent. Thus, the performance requirements were violated when the level of percent correct responding was less than 90 percent correct or greater than 94 percent correct.

These values were chosen for the following reasons: (1) students who have experienced a great deal of failure in reading and reading-associated activities should be placed in a situation where success is frequent and apparent; thus, performance of less than 90 percent correct begins to jeopardize this goal; (2) pilot research in PDI indicates that continual performance of less than 90 percent correct will result in insufficient gains in reading ability; (3) excessively high amounts of correct responding, greater than 94 percent correct, will contribute to boredom on the part of the student; and (4) continual performance above 94 percent correct does not improve the acquisition of target behavior and leads to overtraining.

The variables to be manipulated in order to approximate the target were schedule of reinforcement and amount of work at any one task level. The schedule of reinforcement was as follows: (a) continuous reinforcement, (b) one token for each series of five successive correct responses, (c) one token for each series of ten successive correct responses, and (d) one token for each series of fifteen successive correct responses.

Since TOTE is described in this paper in terms of the Flesch word lists, a brief description of that material is in order. On each page of the Flesch word lists there are five lists of eighteen words each. Every new page introduces a new phonetic element and/or greater word complexity. Thus, each page is operationally defined as a difficulty level.

The options for amount of responding per difficulty level were: reading five word-lists of eighteen words each, reading four word-lists, reading three word-lists, reading two word-lists, reading one word-list, or reading only the review lists covering the previous four difficulty levels but not reading word lists at each difficulty level. The matrix of options generated by these variables is presented in Table 1.

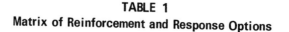

TABLE 1
Matrix of Reinforcement and Response Options

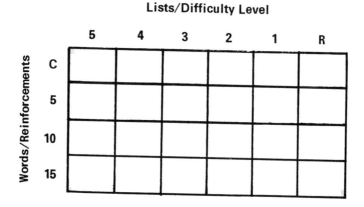

Lists/Difficulty Level

	5	4	3	2	1	R
C						
5						
10						
15						

(Words/Reinforcements)

By definition, the child always starts at continuous reinforcement (C) and five word-lists. After three sessions, he is automatically switched to fifteen successive words per token and three word-lists per difficulty level. From this point forward, all decisions are controlled by the TOTE model. This model is presented in *Figure 1,* which is read in the following manner. A response (reading performance) enters the system and an operation is performed (reinforcement schedule and material). Question 1 is then asked: is the performance level within the range? (Any three successive sessions in which performance is $\ngtr 92 \pm 2$ = a "no" answer). If the answer is yes, then question 2 is asked: is the reading age level up to the target age level?* If the answer is yes, then the decision is to terminate the training. If the answer is no, then the decision is to continue with the original operation.

If the answer to question 1 is no, then question 3 is asked instead of question 2: is the performance above the range? If the answer to this question is yes (three successive sessions in which correct responses exceed 94 percent), then the decision is to advance in the matrix 1 binary unit towards a matrix combination of fifteen words-review or towards the previous level at which the range was violated.

---

*The answer to this question is determined either by the level of the graded reader in which the child is successfully reading, or, more properly, by a standardized test of reading grade level.

This operation would then be performed and the entire series of questions repeated. If the answer to question 3 is no (three successive sessions in which correct responses are less than 90 percent), then the decision is to move the procedures one binary unit towards the matrix combination on which the performance was last within the range. Thus, if the current operation was fifteen words and three lists, and if the answer to question 1 was no, and if the answer to question 3 was yes, then the change would be an advance equal to one-half the distance between fifteen words and three lists, and fifteen words and review. That would be five words and one list. If, subsequently, when that operation was tested and questions 1 and 3 were both answered no, then the change would be one-half the distance between five words and one list, and fifteen words and three lists. This would be ten words and two lists. This same type of management operation would continue throughout the course of the training, in which a combination of binary logic and information theory techniques would be used.

FIGURE 1

Schematic Diagram of the Test-Operate-Test-Execute (TOTE) System Designed for Instructional Management in PDI

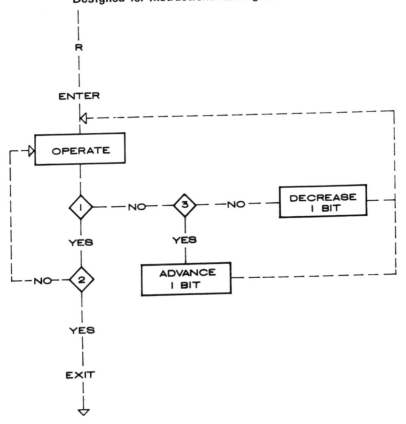

The interface between PDI and its management system, TOTE, is as follows. On any given day, the teacher will execute a training situation under one of the matrix combinations of reinforcement and word lists for a given student. This particular combination is maintained for the entire session. After the session, or sometime prior to the next session, the teacher goes through the TOTE process in order to determine if there should be some change in the combination of reinforcement and word lists used with that student on the occasion of the next training session. In other words, TOTE management decisions are made only between training sessions. During a training session, the teacher merely carries out the results of the TOTE judgment that was made prior to that session.

When the TOTE judgment is either to advance or to decrease procedures, then the binary concept of dividing the remaining alternatives by 50 percent is employed in the matrix to determine which combination of reinforcement and lists is to be used. This particular method is used in an effort to arrive at the appropriate matrix combination as quickly as possible and with as few changes as possible.

It can be seen that the entire judgment process can be handled by a combination of any two of three questions that can be answered yes or no. Appropriate numbers can be coded into the matrix squares and a table can be constructed for ease of interpretation within the matrix. Such a schedule is presented in *Figure 2*. Record keeping for this operation involves only the tabulation (usually in graphic form) of the percent correct responding.

In the case of the sentence-reading task, the process is at a fixed level as mentioned earlier. The child receives a token for each sentence that is read without error. As he continues to read, he begins to encounter material that increases in difficulty as per the graded reader. This, then, is the structure of the system that was designed for remedial reading.

Results

Our experience in PDI (as of this writing) totaled 2100 hours of training. This includes 94,732 word-list responses and 61,754 contextual-sentence responses with N = 100. Calendar time covered is approximately two years. Every three months the data from PDI has been analyzed. Items of major interest are percent correct responding on words, percent correct responding on sentences, and change in reading grade level (measured by a standardized test) per hours of instruction. The intake population profile is that of a child who is nine years of age, in the fourth grade, and reading about one and one-half years below his grade level. There is variation around this description. However, this "mean profile" is reasonably representative.

During the training period for any one child, the teacher records performance information on a daily record chart. *Figure 3* is an example of an individual chart. It can be noted from *Figure 3* that the percent correct responding for words remains around the target range.

FIGURE 2
Matrix System of Variables Used in PDI

TEST	YES	NO
1	2	5
2	3	10
3	4	12
4	16	3
5	6	8
6	7	15
7	1	6
8	14	9
9	8	0
10	13	11
11	10	1
12	3	2
13	2	10
14	5	8
15	6	5
16	–	4
0	1	–

Lists/Difficulty Level

Words/Reinforcements	5	4	3	2	1	R
C	0		6			
5	9	5		11	2	3
10	8		7	10		4
15	14	15	1	13	12	16

The matrix system is based upon the concept of binary units. Each change in the matrix is such that the movement represents one-half the distance between the current point and a finite end point. The table to the left of the matrix is for reference to question 3 of TOTE. Under the "test" heading appear the numbers that refer to the various matrix positions. Under the "yes" heading appear the matrix position numbers that are used if the answer to question 3 is yes. Under the "no" heading appear a similar set of numbers that are used to determine matrix placement if the answer to question 3 is no.

This occurred in the face of performance requirements that were becoming sequentially more difficult. The percent correct responding for sentences shows a gradual increment. This also occurred in the presence of a reading task of increasing difficulty.

In the original sample reported by Gray, Baker and Stancyk,[12] the performance data for 9 Ss was 92.9 percent correct responding on words with σ = 1.9, and 81.1 percent correct responding on sentences. This first sample covered the initial 216 hours of instruction. The data from 14 Ss covered the last 245 hours of instruction (some 1639 hours and 75 Ss after the first sample), and it showed the following results. They had 89.3 percent correct responding on words with σ = .9, and 84.96 percent correct responding on sentences. Statistical analysis indicates that there is no significant difference

FIGURE 3

Performance Chart for One Student

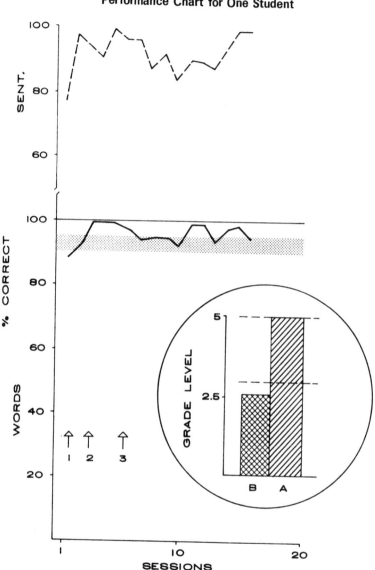

The uppermost graph indicates percent correct sentences, and the lower graph indicates percent correct words. The shaded area through the lower graph represents the target range. The arrows designate points at which TOTE decision was made to change the matrix one position. The inset histogram shows reading grade level before and after 12 hours of PDI. The upper horizontal line in the histogram indicates reading grade level where S should be operating as per age and school placement. The lower horizontal line indicates the level to which initial reading grade level would be expected to advance if it were assumed that reading grade level increased as a function of chronological age.

with p = .05 between any of the reported values. The 14 Ss sampled during the most recent quarter in this study had a population profile similar to the originally reported Ss with age = 9 years, grade level = 4, and reading grade level = 2. The intervening population was similar to these two subpopulations in reported characteristics.

During the first 518 hours of instruction, the change in reading grade level, as measured by the *Gray Oral Reading Tests* paragraphs,[13] was expressed as the linear regression $Y = mX + b$ where m = .0283 and b = .869. This equation was again computed at approximately 1500 hours and the values were m = .0318 and b = .8014. Thus, the change in grade level as a function of training hours remained relatively unchanged. This growth function is graphically illustrated in *Figure 4*.

FIGURE 4
Growth Function of Reading Grade-Level Change Per Hours of Training

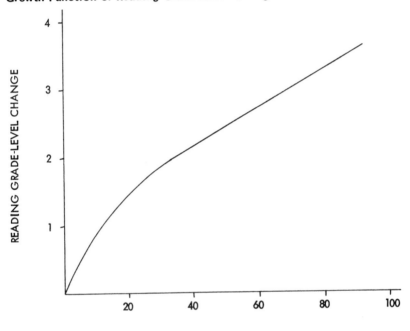

HOURS OF TRAINING

In practical terms this means that for the first 12 hours of training there is an increase in reading grade level of 1.2 years. Thereafter, gains begin to diminish until at 96 hours of training the increase in reading grade level has reached a total of 3.85 years. The greatest σ around this regression = .755 years. One hour of training time is defined as 60 minutes spent in conjunction with one other student in reading training, each of them responding for one-half of the time. In terms of response time the computation of training hours should be divided by one-half. Thus, 1.2 years increment in reading grade level is obtained with 6 hours of response time but with 12 hours of training time. Also, it should be kept in mind that the test used in arriving at the reading grade level has a σ of .5 years.

The data from the last 14 Ss was not included in the computation of the growth function. These 14 Ss had a mean beginning reading grade level of 2 years. They each averaged 38 hours of training, which was distributed over 10 calendar months. Their mean grade-level increase was 1.6 years. Total change, then, was from 2 to 3.6 years reading grade level. The growth function as described in *Figure 4* would have predicted a change of almost 2 years, which would have resulted in a mean reading grade level of 4 years. Thus, the 14 Ss generated a growth function which was .4 years lower than would have been expected in terms of the original growth function. This is well within the standard error reported above.

These data suggest that PDI does generate very consistent data over long periods of time with many students. The data also show that the PDI management system, TOTE, is successful in keeping the percent correct reading scores within acceptable limits of the target range for words.

The Intersect Strategy

The above information suggests that PDI is an efficient and predictable procedure for obtaining improvement in reading grade level. The one significant limitation is its practical maximum gain of between 3.5 and 4.5 years. Educational bureaucracy says that during the early years of school, yearly increments in grade placement will be accompanied by yearly increments in reading grade level. Therefore, increments in reading grade level exist in a one-to-one relationship with grade placement. This straight-line function is noticeably different from the line generated in *Figure 4* for PDI increments per hours of training. This gives rise to a potential problem.

If hours of training are distributed over calendar days so that it takes 12 months to obtain a 2-year gain via PDI, then the effective gain is only 1 year. If the child was originally 2 years behind in reading grade level, then despite the 2-year gain there is still a one-year discrepancy between current reading grade level and the target.

The situation is compounded even further when it is realized that beyond approximately 48 hours of instruction the gain in reading grade level is less in comparison to the first 48 hours. Thus, it would be possible to obtain dramatic gains in reading grade level per hour of instruction only to have this achievement fail to reach the target because the hours of instruction were distributed over too many calendar days. Therefore, only certain options are available to the teacher if he is interested in reaching the target.

Table 2 calculates the number of hours of training needed to achieve the target, given the parameters of grade-level increment needed and the calendar months over which the training is desired. The intersect strategy is only under preliminary analysis, and the figures in the table should be considered as general guidelines rather than as absolute points. As in *Figure 4,* the entries in *Table 2* are in training hours rather than in hours responding.

TABLE 2
Intersect Strategy Matrix

Months To Intersect	GL △						
	1	1.5	2	2.25	2.5	2.75	3
3	12	30	48	54	60	66	78
6	24	36	54	60	72	78	84
9	30	48	60	66	78	84	90
12	42	54	72	78	84	90	104

Major heading (GL△) refers to the distance between the child's measured reading level and his grade placement. Numbers in matrix refer to hours of training. Months to intersect refers to the calendar months in training until intersect is planned. Thus, if a child is 1.5 years below his reading age level and intersect is desired in six months, a total of 36 hours of training must occur for intersect.

Discussion

PDI should be viewed as one example of an effort to effectively implement behavioral strategy in the teaching of reading performance. It was designed for specialized and limited purposes and should be viewed in that perspective. Many different procedures have and can be designed to accomplish similar or related goals in reading. The central idea is to start a student in a reading task in which he will be successful, reinforce the successful performance consistently and immediately, and gradually advance the difficulty of the performance task. One other item could be added to that statement: the reinforcer should be *tangible.* What one uses as a specific tangible reinforcer is not particularly important, so long as it is a reinforcer. It is somewhat doubtful that in PDI the conversion of tokens for M&M's is critical in maintaining the reinforcing properties of the token. What may be more important is the fact that as the training session goes on, the tokens become historical, tangible evidence of having been successful in a reading task.

A child with fifty poker chips stacked up in front of him has visible evidence of success in a performance task that he previously associated with failure and punishment. Nontangible (verbal praise) as well as consumable reinforcers do not provide this added characteristic of historical accounting.

If PDI can be called a program, then it is a program for teacher activity rather than for students or materials. Research findings as well as common experience point up the fact that teacher performance mediates the effect of materials.[14] The good teacher turns out good readers, irrespective of the company who sold the school the reading materials. The poor teacher does little better with "good" materials than with any other materials. The educational-industrial complex keeps the teacher oriented towards materials rather than his classroom behavior. The teacher is looking for the materials that will teach the child to read. Materials should provide the opportunity for the eliciting of certain target responses. The person or the environment then "teaches" by attaching appropriate consequences to the behavioral performance of the student.

In concluding this paper, it might be appropriate to quickly review some characteristics that tend to distinguish this or any behavioral strategy in reading training.

- It is predictable. If a training task has been carefully organized, it will generate a change in skill ability that will follow a reasonably consistent time line. In PDI, 84 percent of all Ss come to within at least .75 years of the growth function in *Figure 4.*

- Its parameters are visible. The variables that are used to modify the response accuracy or response frequency are identified and managed in a predetermined way. The management of the variables, which usually involves both response contingencies and performance difficulty level, is made dependent upon the response performance of the student.

- It is efficient. It responds to the economy of time. This is particularly important in skill areas where the target is chronologically moving away from the starting point. This was pointed out in the discussion of intersect strategy.

- Its effects are definite. It either works or does not work in terms of successful student performance. Management errors on the part of the teacher or the system will cause the student's success rate to drop markedly. Thus, the effects of a procedural error are visible almost as soon as they occur.

- Its procedures are operationally describable. An instructional procedure that has been accurately defined in terms of teacher behavior can be set down in some printed form. Thus, volunteers or instructional technicians can be trained to execute the program. Their results will be no less than the results of the trained professional. The teacher then becomes an instructional manager of several programs that are executed by others.

• And finally, of course, it provides for the proper consequences to be attached to the behavioral performance of the student.

Dr. Lee Meyerson from Arizona State University once told a group of teachers that the laws of learning are like the laws of gravity; they don't cease to operate just because you don't happen to be thinking about them. I think that the implication of Dr. Meyerson's observation is that teachers don't have a choice of whether they will or will not use learning principles in their teaching. They do have the choice of whether to use them deliberately and systematically or whether to use them inadvertently. You could call it a decision to teach on purpose.

NOTES

1. G. L. Bond and R. Dykstra, "The Co-operative Research Program in First Grade Reading Instruction," *Reading Research Quarterly*, 6 (1967), 5-11; T. L. Harris, W. Otto, and C. Barrett, "Summary and Review of Investigations Relating to Reading, July 1, 1966 to June 30, 1967." *Journal of Educational Research*, 61 (1968), 243-264.

2. S. A. Cohen, "Cause vs. Treatment in Reading Achievement," *Journal of Learning Disabilities*, 3 (1970), 43-45.

3. L. Frase, "Questions as Aids to Reading: Some Research and Theory," *American Educational Research Journal*, 5 (1968), 319-332; A. W. Staats et al, "Reinforcement Variables in the Control of Unit Reading Responses," *Journal of Experimental Analysis of Behavior*, 7 (1964), 139-149; A. W. Staats et al, "A Reinforcer System and Experimental Procedure for the Laboratory Study of Reading Acquisition," *Child Development*, 35 (1964), 209-321; A. W. Staats and W. H. Butterfield, "Treatment of Non-Reading in a Culturally Deprived Juvenile Delinquent: An Application of Reinforcement Principles," *Child Development*, 36 (1965), 925-942; C. Whitlock, "Note on Reading Acquisition: An Extension of Laboratory Principles," *Journal of Experimental Child Psychology*, 3 (1966), 83-85; M. M. Wolfe, D. K. Giles, and R. V. Hall, "Experiments with Token Reinforcement in a Remedial Classroom," *Behavior Research and Therapy*, 6 (1968), 51-64.

4. B. Bateman, "A Letter to the Editor in the Critique Section," *Journal of Learning Disabilities*, 2 (1969), 16-17; S. A. Cohen, "Studies in Visual Perception and Reading in Disadvantaged Children," *Journal of Learning Disabilities*, 2 (1969), 8-13; S. A. Cohen, "Cause vs. Treatment."

5. B. B. Gray, R. Baker, and S. Stancyk, "Performance Determined Instruction for Training in Remedial Reading," *Journal of Applied Behavioral Analysis* (in press).

6. B. B. Gray and L. Fygetakis, "Mediated Language Acquisition for Dysphasic Children," *Behavior Research and Therapy*, 6 (1968), 263-280.

7. L. Bloomfield and C. L. Barnhart, *Let's Read (Series)*, (Bronxville, N. Y.: C. L. Barnhart, Inc., 1963); R. Flesch, *Teaching Johnny to Read* (New York, N.Y.: Grosset and Dunlap, 1956).

8. L. R. Goldberg, "Simple Models or Simple Processes? Some Research on Clinical Judgments," *American Psychologist*, 23, No. 7 (1968), 483-496.

9. Ibid, p. 485.

10. G. A. Miller, E. Galenter, and K. H. Pribram, *Plans and the Structure of Behavior*, (New York, N.Y.: Holt, Rinehart & Winston, Inc., 1960).

11. Gray, Baker, and Stancyk, "Performance Determined Instruction."

12. Ibid.

13. W. S. Gray and H. M. Robinson, *Gray Oral Reading Tests* (Indianapolis, Ind.: Bobbs-Merrill Company, Inc., 1963).

14. Bond and Dykstra, "The Co-operative Research Program."

Chapter 2

Language Habilitation
in Children*

Joel Stark

LANGUAGE DEVELOPMENT

T HE INTERACTION of various language systems may be observed
in a two-year-old child's use of language. Coming upon a cluster
of trees in a park, the child may say, "see tee." The phonological
system of most two-year-olds has not matured enough to enable them
to produce certain phonemes proficiently. The likelihood is that the
two-year-old has not learned the singular-plural contrast, *tree* –
trees, or is unable to produce the /z/, which is an additional morpheme because it carries meaning when added to the singular form.
Because of his experience in hearing basic syntactical relations
from adult models, he used the verb *see* before its object, the noun
tree. Finally, he has provided an appropriate semantic category by
calling the huge brown trunk with the little green leaves attached
to it, a *tree*. These language systems interact within the child, but
they are not isolated phenomena; of great importance are the environmental conditions that elicit language responses. It is often only
in the presence of the tree and a listener who reinforces the response that the child is likely to respond at all.

Phonology

Intensive investigations of the development of sound systems
in individual children have been described by W. Leopold, M. M.

---

*The author gratefully acknowledges the assistance of Carol Foster,
Jane Giddan, Robert Gottsleben, and Teris Wright and the encouragement
of Dr. Jon Eisenson. This work was supported in part by funds from the
United States Office of Education (Project 6-8527) and the California
Scottish Rite Foundation. It was done at the Institute for Childhood Aphasia,
Stanford University School of Medicine, California.*

Lewis, and R. Weir.[1] Examination of the child's early progress in sound development suggests that it is not a random process. While the stages are not discrete, the child first cries, coos, and babbles. His "first-word" has a characteristic phonetic shape and is likely to have an objective referent. The sounds that are learned first are often those that seem to require a minimum articulatory effort. Vowel-like sounds will often be produced, which may have evolved as a result of the child lying contented and relaxed after feeding, with mouth open and with the back of his tongue lolling against the soft palate.[2] The relationship of the sounds that the children hear from adult models to their own early sound production is another factor. In addition to ease of effort, it is likely that acoustic cues are used, and more easily perceived sounds are learned first.[3]

R. Jakobson and M. Halle have proposed that universal tendencies exist in the order of the acquisition of sounds.[4] They describe sound categories as configurations that are polar in nature. Hence, all children first have a consonant-vowel (CV) opposition. The first-word is usually a CV unit, which possibly consists of a voiceless unaspirated bilabial stop that is followed by a vowel that covers a wide range around /a/. Even in babbling, phonemic contrasts between fully opened vowels and fully closed stops can be observed. Theoretically, the early development proceeds along a continuum in which the child contrasts a variety of "distinctive features." At the outset the distinction is between vowel and consonant. Then the child contrasts labial consonants with nonlabial consonants and at an early time distinguishes between nasal and oral consonants. Similarly, the vowel system is differentiated on the basis of energy patterns and tongue position. The child that Leopold studied did not establish a front-back vowel opposition until his second year.[5] An analysis of the productions of children based upon the development of sound categories suggests that there is a logic or order to their substitutions, though they may seem bizarre to the adult listener. The child who says [mi] for the word *blanket* may have heard a word with a nasal sound in the middle and produced a sound combination for that word, which contained a nasal. Since acquisition begins in a CV environment, the labial nasal was produced first and was then followed by a front vowel. He has reduced the length of the word and substituted one sound category (nasals) instead of attempting to produce the contrast.

The development of the phonological system does not begin with all of the English phonemes. D. B. Fry has suggested that more consonants are distinguished earlier because their informational loadings are important and there is more pressure for the child to differentiate between them than between the high-intensity vowel sounds.[6] The learning of the system is the result of progressive differentiation of the allowable sound combinations in the particular language.

Morphology

Sounds that carry meaning to a particular lexical item are referred to as morphemes. Thus, the word *dishes* contains five phonemes and two morphemes. The child learns that if he adds /əz/, it means *more than one.* In this case, the plural marker has been subjected to the constraints of the phonological system. To make a plural, we add /əz/ to words that end in sibilant or affricative sounds, whereas we add only /z/ to other voiced sounds and /s/ to voiceless phonemes. Hence, the plural forms of *dish, spoon,* and *fork* have different morphemes or are allomorphs of the same morpheme.

By using nonsense words and cartoon-like drawings, J. Berko studied the child's application of morphological rules under varying phonological conditions.[7] She concluded that preschool and first-grade children operate with clearly delimited rules, and she showed the effect that the phonological system has upon their application. Children tend to overgeneralize these rules at first. For example, with irregular past tenses of verbs such as *ring* and *cling,* children tended to say "ringed" and "clinged," applying a previously learned rule for regular past tenses. With regard to verb inflections, the least amount of difficulty was encountered with the present progressive tense.

Syntax

Investigations of child language development demonstrate that at the earliest time, a child's responses have a certain order and that the child applies rudimentary classes from the outset. K. Brown and C. Fraser call the early productions "telegraphic speech."[8] M. Braine introduced the concept of "pivot" and "open" class words.[9] W. Miller and S. Ervin refer to the child's acquisition of certain "operators."[10] J. J. Jenkins and D. S. Palermo suggest that the child develops a "core of labels."[11]

Each lexical item is combined in a series of permissible ways, which vary from child to child. In Miller and Ervin's studies, one child used the words *on* and *off* as operators or pivots, whereas another child used an identifier type of construction, *thisa—thata* as high-frequency words.[12] A descriptive approach to the development of syntactic competence is succinctly presented by L. Lee.[13] She describes utterances as designative, predicative and fragmentary phrases.

Semantics

In conjunction with the learning of syntax, children assign specific meanings to the verbal symbols they hear and use. The child's previous experience and the isolation of properties or things from his proximate surroundings determine the words he uses. As he progressively distinguishes between stimulus events in the environment, he improves in his ability to classify them and categorize them with verbal labels. L. S. Vygotsky emphasizes the use of words as an integral part of the development of concepts.[14] At first the child unites diverse objects under a common "family name" and then singles out certain common attributes. A young child engages in a considerable amount of experimentation and will tend to use the lexicon inappropriately in many situations.

Semantic development, unlike the structural aspect of language, continues throughout life. While the child of school age may have mastered the language rules, he will always be acquiring new words and refining his ability to employ the ones he already knows. Young children tend to describe events with more "concrete" words, which are directly related to their own actions. They have considerable difficulty in describing their feelings, or in referring to qualities, or in using language to make inferences or projections.

LANGUAGE IMPAIRMENT

Since the primary concern of language habilitation is to improve the child's syntactic, morphophonemic, and semantic abilities, an understanding of the processes involved in normal language development is essential. The developmental and psycholinguistic profiles of language-impaired children suggest that they are by no means a homogeneous group. In addition, by virtue of their own limitations, they do not live in a normal language environment. That is, because the child's language is different from others in the environment, it acts differently on that environment when compared with the language of a child whose speech is functionally more appropriate. The child who fails to respond to speech finds that he is not spoken to.

The language deficits range along a continuum. At the lower end there are the relatively nonverbal children who utter sounds only when crying, coughing, or laughing, to solicit attention. Another characteristic group of children attempts to direct their communication but only succeed in producing jargon. The listener hears an unintelligible, meaningless series of sounds.

The largest group is composed of the ones who produce meaningful language but have a limited repertoire of functional speech. These children have diminutive vocabularies, and their verbal utterances are severely constricted in length. While these children may use language appropriately in social interaction, their speech may be restricted to single CV units. As the length of responses increases, their difficulties in applying morphophonemic and syntactic rules becomes increasingly manifest, and their speech even less functional and intelligible. Words are distorted by the presence of sound substitutions, additions, omissions, or reversals (that is, [nous] for *snow;* [ʃɪs] for *fish)* beyond age expectancy. Phrases are truncated and markedly short (that is, [gap] for *going up;* [pɪsu] for *pretty soon).*

The most severely involved child is totally uncommunicative, detached, and autistic. Sometimes responses are made only to nonlinguistic noises or gross human sounds (for example, when mother shouts "Stop it!"). The sound merely has alerting properties. Some children respond to single lexical items when they are accompanied by gesture or are uttered in the presence of the referent. At higher levels, the child is sometimes able to deal with more "abstract" language but fails to make phonemic discrimination in words (for example, when he is told, "Get your bow...boat...bowl...bone"). Finer morphophonemic nuances such as plural markers and tense changes are not present in their repertoire. The child seems to be unable to deal with the subtle shorthand that constitutes connected speech. Contractions, elisions, and abbreviations are completely confusing. The child only responds appropriately when the language is highly structured and spoken slowly.

If we take into account some of the perceptual problems these children have, we can understand their difficulty with language. In one study with aphasic children, short-term memory for sequences of three lexical items was assessed.[15] Some aphasic children tended to forget the first item by the time the third was uttered, and they made the highest proportion of errors in the first position of the sequence. Hence, it is understandable that the language-impaired child may become confused. By the time he has heard the end of the sentence, he has forgotten the beginning. A relative weakness in auditory perceptual functioning is a common factor. The manifestations are limitations in understanding and using language.

CLINICAL MANAGEMENT

In order to modify language behavior and make it more functional, we have used programed learning procedures. Essentially, the programed approach requires that the *likelihood of errors be markedly reduced*. The clinician provides a controlled, distraction-free environment in which *observable responses emitted by the child are reinforced immediately*. It is of paramount importance that the stimulus materials be presented in a carefully graded manner so as to insure successful responding.

The child's responses determine the nature and direction of the program as well as the rate at which the teaching proceeds. We attempt to use those stimuli to which the child gives evidence of responding appropriately. More specific suggestions regarding the construction of programs may be found in R. H. Gottsleben et al.[16]

For some children, emphasis on visual stimuli has been most effective, possibly because, unlike auditory stimuli, visual stimuli are in the child's presence over a period of time. With children who do not emit verbal behavior, a designative response mode is used (for example, having the child point to or match pictures).

At first the stimuli may be pictures of common-count nouns (for example, pictures of a ball, tree, and car) to which the child matches the written word. Then the number of word classes is expanded. In effect, the child learns to "read" single words and then units that include verbs, auxiliaries, objective clauses, and prepositional phrases. New lexical items are added only after the child has responded appropriately to earlier ones. The stimuli are presented in a manner that teaches the *order of the constituents of a sentence*, particularly the subject-verb-object relations.

It would be naive to assume that even for the most severely aphasic child, training is restricted to the use of visual stimuli. The building of responses to visual stimuli at the outset increases the probability of success. At the same time, the clinician provides the child with auditory experiences that are less demanding than those for which he is likely to have had a history of failure. For example, early in the training program we may teach a child to respond to the presence of sound. We would then introduce a discrimination between two sounds that have grossly different distinctive features, both visually and auditorily. Earliest discrimination is often between a labial such as /m/ or /p/, and the open vowel /a/. The child may respond to visual differences but these can be gradually faded.*

Stimulus-Response Modes

A major requisite, which underlies and guides all of the training procedures, is that the clinician must have an awareness of, and appreciation for, the specific nature of the stimulus and the response. Visual stimuli can be: body gestures; pictures; three-dimensional objects and forms varying in size, shape, and color; facial movements that accompany sound; or graphic representations. Similarly, responses can be made in the form of pointing, pressing levers, writing, or saying. If the activity includes a visual-pictorial stimulus with a designated response, the child may match or sort pictures. At first the stimulus items are likely to be identical pictures. Then he may be presented with pictures that are similar but not identical, which requires that he must, for example, sort two differently shaped chairs and two different makes of cars. On this basis, categories can be developed according to function, so that the concept of *furniture*, which stands for a variety of things that have many different specific labels, can be taught visually.

Many modifications of the approach are possible. Auditory cues may be used to advantage. The child may be presented with an auditory-verbal stimulus and respond by pointing to the appropriate picture card (designated pictorial response). Language units may be taught through speech reading, in which the child learns to associate the facial movements of the clinician with a picture and selects the one appropriate to the facial movement the clinician produces. If the child's responses are incorrect, the clinician may

---

*In another paper (J. Stark, J. J. Giddan, and J. Meisel, "Increasing Verbal Behavior in an Autistic Child," *Journal of Speech and Hearing Disorders*, 33 (1968), 42-48), we described the way in which a repertory of sounds was used to build a core of verbal labels.

use written forms of the word as well. Often the clinician will have the child copy the printed word that accompanies a picture. The prime consideration is that the stimuli used are those to which the child will respond appropriately.

Critical Elements in Language Learning

Language consists of units that are manipulated or "transformed" according to certain rules in a variety of ways. Even the two-word constructions of two-year-old children have a grammatical system.[17] Children with functionally appropriate language have learned that nouns are preceded by determiners rather than followed by them (*this chair*, not *chair this*); that word classes have a semantic consistency; and that each class of words has certain privileges of occurrence within a phrase (*want the toy*, not *toy want the*).

When applied to syntactic development, the construct of critical elements may be defined as one in which *certain words or semantic units within a phrase differentiate that phrase in meaning.* In the sentences, "The boy is riding the wagon" and "The girl is pulling the wagon," the critical elements are the nouns, *boy – girl* and the verbs, *riding – pulling.* The child must respond to both of these distinctions when matching printed word-cards to pictures depicting these phrases. If the child places a word-card of a boy pulling a wagon below a picture of a boy riding a wagon, it is immediately evident to the clinician that the misunderstood critical element is the verb. At this point, a review of the verb distinctions would be presented. The terminal behavior may be the discrimination of parts of an active declarative sentence, such as "The boy is sleeping on the bed." Here, correct responses to the noun phrases, the verb, and the preposition should be elicited singly and in combination. In such a sentence there are four critical elements that need to be responded to appropriately.

Figure 1 shows a possible hierarchy of stimulus events that may serve as a guide for language programing. In a lower-level program, the child has to respond discriminatively to three critical elements — color, number, and noun — in a word-card to picture-card matching task. The materials include color chips, and three-by-five-inch index cards printed with numerals, color patches, pictures, or typewritten words. The child and the clinician sit at a table that contains a slot-board into which the index cards can be placed. The clinician presents the stimulus items to the child and records the responses he makes. Correct responses are reinforced by verbal approval, candies, trinkets, or tokens. The nature of the reinforcer used depends upon the response of the child. For some, the clinician may smile, say "Good boy," and proceed to the next stimulus item; for others, social approval is paired with a reinforcer such as food or candy.

At the outset, the stimuli are the nouns *car, ball,* and *tree.* The clinician hands the child a single word-card, which is to be matched

FIGURE 1

A Hierarchy of Simulus Events

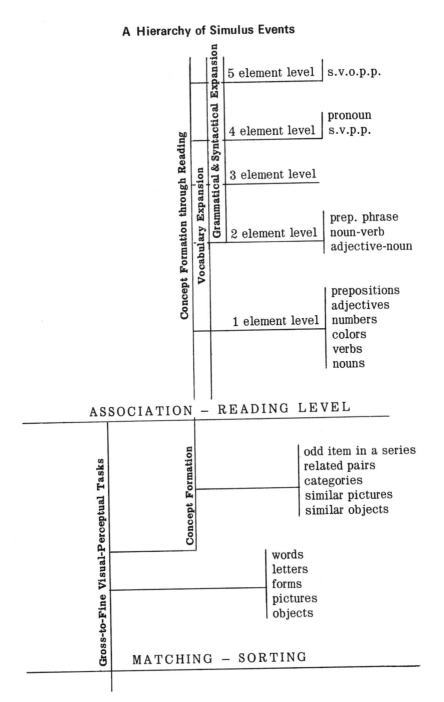

to a single picture-card. Then two picture-cards are placed on the slot-board and the word-cards are randomly presented to the child who matches them. The clinician may present one noun and vary the color, or he may keep the color constant and vary the noun. A twelve-card matrix can be built from the four colors and three nouns in this program. If the child makes an error, the clinician may:

- Reduce the number of stimulus items.

- Alter the nature of the stimulus or the response (have him point and say).

- Review either noun or color labels as in an earlier step in the program.

When three critical elements are presented in phrases such as "two green balls," the matrix can include thirty-six items. Hence, there is a gradual progression to establish a longer and more complex repertoire.

The programing of stimuli and recording of responses is one way in which we can evaluate the clinical process. The variables that complicate such studies are the different reinforcers, clinicians, physical environments, and extension of the responses to more functional language environments. In addition, many tend to view programing as a sterile method in which the clinician serves as an automaton who rigidly adheres to specifically prescribed procedures.

We have found that many clinicians are able to use the programs as a guide for therapy. Within this framework, they are able to make modifications and impose whatever creativity they feel is necessary. The programs represent a graded, orderly, and effective way to teach a specific behavior. To illustrate the nature of a program, the following is the description of the first part of an "animal" program:

Materials: Board, approximately eighteen by thirty inches with six slots to hold three-by-five-inch pictures and word-cards.

Stimuli: Pictures and typewritten words of the nouns *bunny, cat, dog,* and *horse.*

Responses: Correct response in all frames is to match the word-cards to the pictures. The clinician removes each word-card immediately after the child places it.

FRAME 1.

Procedure: a) Place dog picture at top of slot-board (pocket #1).
b) Demonstrate: Place dog word-card next to dog picture.
c) Remove dog word-card and hand it to child.

FRAME 2.

Stimuli on board: dog picture and word-card (pocket #1).

Procedure: a) Place bunny picture in pocket #2, below dog picture.
b) Demonstrate: Place bunny word-card next to

bunny picture.

   c) Remove bunny word-card and hand it to child.

FRAME 3.

Stimuli on board: dog (pocket #1) and bunny (pocket #2) pictures.

Procedure: Hand dog and bunny word-cards to child, in random order, one at a time.

FRAME 4.

Stimuli on board: bunny picture (pocket #1) and dog picture (pocket #2).

Procedure: Same as Frame 3.

FRAME 5.

Stimuli on board: bunny picture and word-card (pocket #1), dog picture and word-card (pocket #2), horse picture (pocket #3).

Procedure: Demonstrate: Place horse word-card next to horse picture and hand it to child.

FRAME 6.

Stimuli on board: bunny picture and word-card (pocket #1), dog picture (pocket #2), horse picture (pocket #3).

Procedure: Hand horse and dog word-cards to child, in random order, one at a time.

FRAME 7.

Stimuli on board: bunny picture (pocket #1), dog picture (pocket #2), horse picture (pocket #3).

Procedure: Hand bunny, dog, and horse word-cards to child, in random order, one at a time.

FRAME 8.

Stimuli on board: horse picture (pocket #1), bunny picture (pocket #2), dog picture (pocket #3).

Procedure: Hand bunny, dog, and horse word-cards to child, in random order, one at a time.

FRAME 9.

Stimuli on board: horse picture and word-card (pocket #1), bunny picture and word-card (pocket #2), dog picture and word-card (pocket #3), cat picture (pocket #4).

Procedure: Demonstrate: Place cat word-card next to picture, remove it, and hand it to child.

FRAME 10.

Stimuli on board: horse picture and word-card (pocket #1), bunny picture (pocket #2), dog picture and word-card (pocket #3), cat picture (pocket #4).

Procedure: Hand cat and bunny word-cards to child, in random order, one at a time.

FRAME 11.

Stimuli on board: horse picture (pocket #1), bunny picture and word-card (pocket #2), dog picture (pocket #3), cat picture (pocket #4).

Procedure: Hand horse, dog, and cat word-cards to child, in random order, one at a time.

FRAME 12.

Stimuli on board: horse picture (pocket #1), bunny picture (pocket #2), dog picture (pocket #3), cat picture (pocket #4).

Procedure: Hand the four word-cards to the child, in random order, one at a time.

The second part of the program requires the child to combine the auxiliary *can* with the verbs *eat, sleep,* and *walk.* In the last part of the program, the required performance is to respond appropriately to noun-verb combinations. Criterion performance for most of the frames is four out of five correct responses when there is more than one stimulus item to be discriminated.

For some children it is not necessary to present all of the frames in order for them to respond appropriately to the desired terminal behavior. For others it is helpful when the clinician adds an auditory stimulus or reviews earlier steps. Hence, modifications can be made in this or other programs that are based upon an analysis of the child's responses.

WE ARE WELL AWARE that unless the material that constitutes the terminal behavior of the program becomes functional for the child, its efficacy is questionable. This is a major criticism that is directed toward programed learning. Wherever possible, provisions are made for "carryover." For example, during the holiday season many clinicians administer a program that enables a child to describe the decorating of a Christmas tree and similar events in which he is likely to participate. In conjunction with the "animal" program, the clinician will introduce the animal labels in other contexts and have the child observe and feed a pet at home. To date, we have been encouraged by the many responses that have become functional for these children. The above procedures are just one aspect of the training. I have described the way in which language-impaired children can learn the order of the constituents of a phrase, and in our work at the institute we have been encouraged by the results of such a program of clinical management. We also recognize that there is much that is yet to be known about language development and habilitation.

NOTES

1. W. Leopold, *Speech Development of a Bilingual Child*, 4 vols. (Evanston, Ill.: Northwestern University Studies, 1939-1949); M. L. Lewis, *Infant Speech*, 2d ed. (London: Routledge and Kegan Paul, Ltd., 1951); R. Weir, *Language in a Crib* (The Hague: Morton & Co., 1962).

2. Lewis, *Infant Speech.*

3. D. B. Fry, "Development of the Phonological System in the Normal and the Deaf Child," *The Genesis of Language,* eds. F. Smith and G. Miller (Cambridge, Mass.: The MIT Press, 1966).

4. R. Jakobson and M. Halle, "Phonemic Patterning," *Psycholinguistics,* ed. S. Saporta (New York, N.Y.: Holt, Rinehart, and Winston, 1961), pp. 346-358.

5. Leopold, *Speech Development of a Bilingual Child.*

6. Fry, "Development of the Phonological System."

7. J. Berko, "The Child's Learning of English Morphology," *Word,* 14 (1958), 150-177.

8. K. Brown and C. Fraser, "The Acquisition of Syntax," *The Acquisition of Language,* eds. V. Bellugi and R. Brown, *Monographs of the Society for Research in Child Development,* Serial No. 92, 29 (1964).

9. M. Braine, "The Ontogeny of English Phrase Structure: The First Phrase," *Language,* 39 (1963), 1-13.

10. W. Miller and S. Ervin, "The Development of Grammar in Child Language," *The Acquisition of Language,* eds. V. Bellugi and R. Brown, *Monographs of the Society for Research in Child Development,* Serial No. 92, 29 (1964).

11. J. J. Jenkins and D. S. Palermo, "Mediation Processes and the Acquisition of Linguistic Structure," *The Acquisition of Language,* eds. V. Bellugi and R. Brown, *Monographs of the Society for Research in Child Development,* Serial No. 92, 29 (1964).

12. Miller and Ervin, "The Development of Grammar."

13. L. Lee, "Developmental Sentence Types: A Method for Comparing Normal and Deviant Syntactic Development," *Journal of Speech and Hearing Disorders,* 31 (1966), 311-330.

14. L. S. Vygotsky, *Thought and Language* (Cambridge, Mass.: The MIT Press, 1962).

15. J. Stark, R. Poppen, and M. May, "Effects of Alteration of Prosidic Features on the Sequencing Performance of Aphasic Children," *Journal of Speech and Hearing Disorders,* 10 (1967), 849-855.

16. R. H. Gottsleben et al., "Developmental Language Programs for Aphasic Children," *Academic Therapy,* 3, No. 4 (1968), 278-282.

17. V. Bellugi and R. Brown (eds.), *The Acquisition of Language, Monographs of The Society for Research in Child Development,* Serial No. 92, 29 (1964).

Chapter 3

Attention Span:
An Operant
Conditioning Analysis

Garry L. Martin
Richard B. Powers

Reprinted by permission of the authors and *Exceptional Children*, April 1967

CONTEMPORARY literature suggests that the concept of attention span refers to two different phenomena. Under "span of attention," H. B. English and Ava C. English list: (a) The number of distinct objects that can be perceived in a single momentary presentation; and (b) the length of time a person can attend to one thing.[1] The first of these two definitions has historical precedent over the second. It relates to one of the oldest questions in the field of experimental psychology, namely, how many things can we attend to in a single instant of time?

The second definition, the more recent and frequent usage of the concept, is the one with which this paper is concerned. The length of time a person can attend to one thing was initially referred to as voluntary attention.[2] More recently, the length of time a subject concentrated on a task has been referred to variously as interest span,[3] sustained attention,[4] occupation interest,[5] perseveration,[6] or, most usually, as attention span.[7]

With respect to special populations, it was suggested as early as 1904 that, "alienists and specialists in nervous disorders inform us that mental disease is commonly accompanied by disturbance in the power of attention."[8] The concept of short attention span was suggested by E. Kuhlman as a way of accounting for the retardate's apparent difficulty in discrimination learning.[9] Recently, A.A. Strauss and his associates have been influential in stressing the difficulty of brain injured children in attending to a task for any length of time, [10] and references to the short attention span of retardates are common in the contemporary literature. [11]

Although the attention span concept appears to be widely employed in psychological and educational literature on special populations, current usage of the term is not entirely consistent. Some of these inconsistencies will be discussed briefly in the following section.

Current Usage

The concept seems to be used currently in at least three major ways. First, empirical evidence indicates that "attention span" is task specific. Measurements with normal children have yielded values ranging from seconds to forty-five minutes. [12] K. E. Moyer and B. von Haller Gilmer concluded that to speak of the concept of a "mean attention span" for children was meaningless because its measure depended so much on selecting the right task for the right age child. They proposed the notion of attention spans to replace that of attention span. Their point is well taken and might profitably be applied to the concept of a short attention span for retardates. That is, it seems reasonable that attention span measures of retardates are also task and child specific, and not a characteristic of retardation per se.

Second, although several authors have talked as though short attention span, distractibility, and hyperactivity refer to different phenomena, differences among the behavioral referents of these concepts are often difficult to specify. For example, concerning the brain injured child, Strauss and Kephart wrote:

> He finds it impossible to engage in any activity in a concentrated fashion, but is always being led aside from the task at hand by stimuli which should remain extraneous but do not....Under these conditions it would be expected that the individual would tend to respond to a variety of extraneous stimuli and lose track of the task at hand. We would describe such behavior as "distractibility." [13]

In their report on research in activity level, R. L. Cromwell et al. stated:

> Another paramount problem is that activity level, owing to its lack of clarity in definition, can be confused with other variables. For example, the subject with a short attention span who shifts quickly from one goal-directed activity to another may appear to the observer to have a higher rate of activity than a subject fixated at one task but exerting the same amount of activity. [14]

In view of such statements, a reader might refer to a child who engages in a task for a brief period of time as having a short attention span, or being easily distractible, or showing superactivity. Yet the concepts are discussed as though they were distinct phenomena.

For example, in their article on activity level, Cromwell et al. wrote:

According to their (Strauss' and his associates') conception of the brain-injured child, an environment of overstimulation should exaggerate the symptoms of distractible behavior, short attention span, and superactivity. [15]

If these concepts do refer to different behavioral phenomena, the differences are not always obvious.

Third, attention span is sometimes discussed as though it were a faculty or process and the observed behaviors are considered as symptoms of the underlying short attention span. A consequence of this approach is the tendency to refer to short attention span as an absolute, unchanging characteristic of mental retardation. In some cases, a very short attention span is simply cited as a characteristic of the mentally retarded with no elaboration offered. [16] In other cases, it is used as a diagnostic device to distinguish categories of mental retardation. [17]

A major consequence of these usages of short attention span is that they tend to impede the education of the retarded. A "rigid attention span" can be easily invoked as a way of accounting for poor attending behavior. But paying attention is a prerequisite in all classroom situations. Thus, as others have observed, [18] various educational activities are often not attempted with a particular retarded child simply because his short attention span is thought to interfere with the necessary task attendance.

An Operant Conditioning
Analysis of Attention Span

An operant conditioning analysis of attention span suggests an alternative view. This approach offers powerful tools which can be used to manipulate the length of time a child attends to a particular task. The most important single principle of operant conditioning is the empirical principle of reinforcement. The principle refers to the observation that there are certain environmental events (commonly called rewards) that we will work to produce. We influence others with these events when we reward any behavior that we wish to make more frequent. These rewarding events are more technically referred to as reinforcers. A reinforcer is defined as a stimulus, the presentation of which, following a response, increases the probability of future occurrence of that response. The common sense notion of reward is certainly not new. What is new is the precise specification of several variables that are crucial to the success of the reinforcement procedure.

The first crucial variable is the contingent relationship between the response and the reinforcer. The contingency is a logical if-then relationship, which is to be distinguished from a simple pleasant or rewarding situation in which a person might find himself. A pleasant situation typically doesn't require the person to do anything. The reinforcement procedure, however, requires the occurrence of some specified response prior to the presentation of a reinforcer. The second crucial variable is the immediacy of reinforcement. To be most effective, the reinforcer must follow the response without delay. A more extensive discussion of operant conditioning techniques may be found in M. Sidman and in J. L. Michael.[19]

In this framework, the term "attention span" refers to nothing more than the behavioral events to which the name is attached. These behavioral events are explained in terms of environmental variables in the presence of which the behavior occurs. This interpretation places emphasis upon behavior that interferes with attending to a task, as well as the attending behavior itself. Thus, task perseverance, or a long attention span, is primarily a function of presenting reinforcement contingent upon attending behavior, and allowing incompatible behavior to go unreinforced. On the other hand, short attention span is observed when reinforcement is contingent upon behavior that is incompatible with attending to the task of interest, and attending behavior goes unreinforced. A similar analysis has been made by Michael in a discussion of the relevance of animal research to problems of learning in the retarded.[20]

An experiment conducted by the authors supports this analysis. The purpose of the experiment was to study the effects of novel human stimuli upon an operant response in retarded children[21]. The experimental chamber was divided into two cubicles separated by a plexiglass partition that allowed visual and auditory feedback. Each cubicle contained a lever mounted on a table. The children were conditioned individually to operate a lever; that is, when the child pressed the lever, a token fell into a token cup. The token could then be exchanged for either salty foods (popcorn, pretzels, peanuts, etc.) or juice immediately after its receipt. Gradually, the number of lever presses required was increased until the schedule of reinforcement was a fixed ratio 10 (every tenth response was reinforced). The subjects were exposed to this schedule until they achieved a stable performance for five consecutive sessions. Each daily session lasted twenty minutes or until the subject received fifty reinforcements.

At this point a confederate was introduced into the opposing cubicle with instructions to do one of three things: A, sit quietly and read a book; B, operate the lever and receive food or juice on a fixed interval thirty-second schedule of reinforcement (the first response after thirty seconds produced the reinforcement); C, operate the lever and receive a token for every thirtieth response (fixed ratio 30). The token was then exchanged for food or juice.

These three conditions of the confederate were introduced on the assumption that each varied with respect to the frequency and intensity of the auditory and visual stimuli they provided to the subject. Two subjects were exposed to condition C; one was given condition A and B in that order; and the other subject was exposed to the sequence A, B, C. When more than one condition was used, the subject was returned to the control condition (fixed ratio 10) for a session prior to the onset of each new test condition.

In all three test conditions, the introduction of the confederate produced a temporary disruption of the stable pattern of responding that was observed under the control conditions. However, this stable pattern of responding was recovered, indicating that adaptation to the stimuli presented by the confederate had occurred.

Observations made during the initial conditioning sessions and during the test sessions have direct relevance to the issue of attention span. During the first four conditioning sessions, no subject earned the fifty reinforcements within the allotted time of twenty minutes. Failure to earn all available reinforcements appeared to be due to the frequent occurrence of responses that were incompatible with lever pressing such as climbing, crouching, banging on the door, lying on the floor, and so on. In other words, the subjects might have been described as shifting quickly from one goal directed activity to another, and many persons undoubtedly would have been willing to use the notion of a short attention span as an explanation for the subject's failure to respond in a consistent manner on the lever. Yet, by the fourth session, the subjects came to "pay attention" to the task for the duration of the session, earning their fifty reinforcements within the twenty-minute period. This was accomplished by reinforcing only the task of concern and ignoring other incompatible behavior.

Some authors have suggested that subjects with a short attention span for a certain event or activity often invent activities with greater appeal to them.[22] Relevant to this suggestion are the observations taken during the test sessions. The disruption of the stable pattern of responding in the presence of the confederate was due to the occurrence of activities that are incompatible with lever pressing, such as staring, pointing, laughing at the other person, or tapping on the plexiglass partition. It might be suggested that the subjects invented these activities because of their greater appeal, since the only evidence ever offered for this explanation is the fact of their occurrence. However, such an explanation adds nothing in the way of correction procedures. By ignoring these activities and reinforcing only the lever pressing task, the subjects came to pay attention even in the face of the variety of visual and auditory stimuli provided by the confederate. A recent report indicates that even the occurrence of an earthquake in the middle of an experiment failed to disrupt the attending behavior of a retarded subject when that behavior was reinforced.[23]

Observations reported by other authors support this analysis. Nancy Kerr worked with two brain-injured girls who supposedly had short attention spans and were irresponsible and hyperactive in the classroom (the hospital staff had reported the girls to have such short attention spans that they could not attend to a particular task for longer than three to six minutes).[24] Kerr devised the task of folding two-by-five-inch cards along a dotted line and placing each folded card in a container. During the first session the usual or traditional technique of urging the child to continue was used whenever a lag in productivity occurred, i.e., the experimenter would say such things as, "Come on, you can do better than that," and approximately ten minutes of productive behavior was obtained. During the next two sessions, experimenter attention was made contingent upon task performance, in the manner dictated by the empirical principles of reinforcement, and a full hour of work was obtained each time. Two more sessions of the traditional technique and two more reinforcement sessions replicated these effects. In discussing these results, Kerr reported:

> The significance of a demonstration that attention span of brain damaged children can be increased through manipulation of reinforcement variables is quite obvious. Procedures which induce a child to attend to a task facilitate education, therapies, and even physical examination. For example, a question about the eyesight of one of the children in this study had been raised by other staff members. An attempt to have her eyes examined was unsuccessful, "because of her short attention span." However, in the present experiment, it was easily determined that she could discriminate the fine printed line along which the paper was to be folded. Had the goal been to test her vision, other visual tasks could have been presented. [25]

So far, emphasis has been placed upon the reinforcement of attending behavior. In addition, an operant analysis also stresses a concern for environmental variables that maintain behavior incompatible with a long attention span. For example, several staff members from the institution where the authors' research was conducted had commented upon the short attention spans of their students as a major barrier to their education. However, observation of these students in their respective classrooms revealed that they received attention from the teacher only when they left their desks, cried, or, in short, emitted behavior that was incompatible with a long attention span.

Evidence supporting the importance of reinforcement principles in eliminating behavior that is incompatible with attending to a task comes from two recent experiments. Elaine H. Zimmerman and J. Zimmerman eliminated unproductive classroom behavior in two emotionally disturbed boys by removing social consequences of the behavior. [26] In both cases, the student would respond to a teacher's request by emitting behavior that was incompatible with the task of concern (such as having temper tantrums, emitting irrelevant verbal behavior, and talking baby talk). The experimenter initially responded to such behavior, giving the subject much attention and encouragement to respond appropriately. As this approach proved unsuccessful, the experimenter next proceeded to give attention (reinforcement) in the form of smiling, chatting, and physical proximity only after the emission of desired classroom behavior, or some approximation of it in the desired direction. As a result of this treatment, the students soon came to attend to the teacher's questions and classroom tasks.

J. S. Birnbrauer, S. W. Bijou, and M. Wolf, [27] selected eight boys from the youngest and educationally most naive educable children from the Rainier School for Retarded Children in an effort to teach them for a school year, using programed instruction and reinforcement techniques exclusively. With these techniques, the investigators had a great deal of success in teaching primary academic subjects and related practical skills. Relevant to this discussion, they report:

Behavior problems did arise frequently and were handled almost exclusively with extinction; i.e., they were simply ignored. The physical arrangement of the room and the staggered schedules permitted temper tantrums, for example, to "wear themselves out" without overly affecting the other pupils. Shortly after the pupil stopped the inappropriate behavior, he received attention. In other words, adult attention was reserved for socially acceptable behavior.[28]

Under these conditions, the retarded students came to read for twenty minutes at a time with the teacher, work quietly at their desks at various tasks, and even do homework.

An operant conditioning approach considers attention span only in terms of the time spent engaging in a task, and uses reinforcement variables in accounting for task persistence. This approach provides teachers with a powerful tool with which to strengthen good attending behavior.

NOTES

1. H. B. English and Ava C. English, *A Comprehensive Dictionary of Psychological and Psychoanalytic Terms* (New York, N.Y.: McGraw-Hill, 1963).

2. W. James, *The Principles of Psychology*, Vol. 1 (New York, N.Y.: Henry Holt, 1890); J. R. Angell, *Psychology* (New York, N.Y.: Henry Holt, 1904).

3. A. Herring and H. L. Koch, "A Study of Some Factors Influencing the Interest Span of Preschool Children," *Journal of Genetic Psychology*, 38 (1930), 249-279.

4. H. S. Schacter, "A Method for Measuring the Sustained Attention of Preschool Children, *Journal of Genetic Psychology*, 43 (1933), 339-371.

5. K. M. B. Bridges, "Occupational Interests of Three-Year-Old Children," *Journal of Genetic Psychology*, 34 (1927), 415-423.

6. H. M. Cushing, "A Perseverative Tendency in Preschool Children; a Study in Personality Differences," *Archives of Psychology*, 108 (1929).

7. D. L. Cockrell, "A Study of the Play of Children of Preschool Age by an Unobserved Observer," *Genetic Psychology Monographs*, 17 (1935), 377-469; H. Bott, "Observation of Play Activities in a Nursery School," *Genetic Psychology Monographs*, 4 (1928), 44-88; D. Van Alstyne, *Play Behavior and Choice of Play Materials of Preschool Children* (Chicago, Ill.: University of Chicago Press, 1932); M. V. Gutteridge, *The Duration of Attention in Young Children*. Australian Council of Educational Research, Melbourne University Educational Research Series, No. 41, Oxford University Press, 1935; K. E. Moyer and B. von Haller Gilmer, "Attention Spans of Children for Experimentally Designed Toys," *Journal of Genetic Psychology*, 87 (1955), 187-201.

8. Angell, *Psychology*, p. 80.

9. E. Kuhlman, "Experimental Studies in Mental Deficiency," *American Journal of Psychology*, 15 (1904), 391-446.

10. A. A. Strauss and L. Lehtinen, *Psychopathology and Education of the Brain-Injured Child*, Vol. 1 (New York, N.Y.: Grune and Stratton, 1947); A. A. Strauss and N. Kephart, *Psychopathology and Education of the Brain-Injured Child*, Vol. 2 (New York, N.Y.: Grune and Stratton, 1955).

11. Harriet E. Blodgett and Grace J. Warfield, *Understanding Mentally Retarded Children* (New York, N.Y.: Appleton-Century-Crofts, 1959); H. Goldstein and Dorothy M. Seigle, "Characteristics of Educable Mentally Handicapped Children," *Mental Retardation*, ed. J. H. Rothstein (New York, N.Y.: Holt, Rinehart and Winston, 1961), pp. 204-230; R. L. Cromwell, A. Baumeister, and W. Hawkins, "Research in Activity Level," *Handbook of Mental Deficiency*, ed. N. R. Ellis (New York, N.Y.: McGraw-Hill, 1963), pp. 632-663; E. W. Weber, *Mentally Retarded Children and their Education* (Springfield, Ill.: Charles C Thomas, 1964); Malinda D. Garton, *Teaching the Educable Mentally Retarded* (Springfield, Ill.: Charles C Thomas, 1964).

12. Moyer and Gilmer, "Attention Spans of Children."

13. Strauss and Kephart, *Psychopathology and Education*, p. 135.

14. Cromwell, Baumeister, and Hawkins, "Research in Activity Level," p. 634.

15. Ibid., p. 641.

16. Weber, *Mentally Retarded Children*.

17. Blodget and Warfield, *Understanding Mentally Retarded Children*.

18. R. S. Lewis, A. A. Strauss, and L. E. Lehtinen, *The Other Child* (New York, N.Y.: Grune and Stratton, 1960).

19. M. Sidman, "Operant Techniques," *Experimental Foundations of Clinical Psychology*, ed. A. J. Bachrach (New York, N.Y.: Basic Books, 1962), pp. 170-210; J. L. Michael, "Guidance and Counseling as the Control of Behavior," *Guidance in American Education: Backgrounds and Prospects* (Cambridge, Mass.: Harvard Graduate School of Education, 1964).

20. J. L. Michael, "The Relevance of Animal Research." Paper presented at a symposium on language learning in the mentally retarded, University of Kansas, Lawrence, 1963.

21. G. L. Martin and R. B. Powers, "Social Disruption of an Operant Response in Retardates." Paper presented at American Association for the Advancement of Science, Flagstaff, Arizona, 1965.

22. Goldstein and Seigle, "Characteristics of Educable Mentally Handicapped Children."

23. H. Sloane and L. J. Harper, "Experimental Control During an Earthquake," *Journal of Experimental Analysis of Behavior*, VIII (1965), 425-426.

24. Nancy Kerr, "Applications of Behavioristic Techniques and Field Theoretical Concepts in Somatopsychology." Unpublished doctoral dissertation (Houston, Tex.: University of Houston, 1962).

25. Ibid, p. 118.

26. Elaine H. Zimmerman and J. Zimmerman, "The Alteration of Behavior in a Special Classroom Situation," *Journal of Experimental Anslysis of Behavior*, 5 (1962), 59-60.

27. J. S. Birnbrauer, S. W. Bijou, and M. Wolf, "Programmed Instruction in the Classroom," *Case Studies in Behavioral Modification*, eds. L. P. Ullmann and L. Krasner (New York, N.Y.: Holt, Rinehart and Winston, 1965), pp. 358-363.

28. Ibid.

III

Programs in Operation:

BEHAVIOR MODIFICATION

MODELS AND CURRICULUM IN THE CLASSROOM

T HIS FINAL SECTION presents a description of four distinctly different behavior-modification programs that have proven to be effective wtih learning-disability children. In Chapter 1, McKenzie et al., working on the assumption that teachers can more readily accept behavior-modification principles if the rewards used are the more traditional ones to which they have become accustomed, describe a program in which the normal grading system has been combined with a secondary reinforcement of money to enhance the strength of grades as reinforcement for academic improvement in learning-disability children.

Hewett continues to be one of the major behavior-modification theorists in the country today. Just as his engineered classroom concept provided one of the earliest and most clearly defined applications of behavioral principles to special classes for disturbed children, the Learning Center program presented in Chapter 2 by Hewett, et al., will provide a major bridge to returning the special child to regular classroom programs and away from the rigid categorization procedures that have tended to develop in special education over the past two decades.

In Chapter 3, Nolen, Kunzelmann, and Haring describe a program that proved to be effective with children ranging in age from twelve to sixteen with severe learning and behavior disorders. The major emphasis of this program is concerned with the utilization of the

Premack principle, in which highly desirable activities are made available contingent upon academic performance.

The final chapter, by myself and Criner, presents the results of the first year of a program in which Precision Teaching procedures were utilized to modify the behavior of emotionally disturbed and learning-disability children ranging in age from six to nine. This article also provides additional support for Lovitt's suggestion in Chapter 1, Section I, that dynamic behavioral assessment provides the most effective means available for the understanding of a given child's learning difficulties in a dynamic and changing daily environment.

Chapter 1

Behavior Modification of Children with Learning Disabilities Using Grades as Tokens and Allowances as Backup Reinforcers

Hugh S. McKenzie
Marilyn Clark
Montrose M. Wolf
Richard Kothera
Cedric Benson

Reprinted by permission of the authors and *Exceptional Children*, Summer 1968

A NUMBER of investigations have indicated that behavior modification techniques can be highly effective in the beneficial change of social and academic behaviors of both normal and exceptional children. Recent research has applied these techniques to bright, preschool children;[1] to school dropouts;[2] to emotionally disturbed children;[3] and to low achieving culturally deprived children.[4] More extensive reviews of this growing body of experimental literature are given by R. C. Anderson and R. J. Whelan.[5] The approach that these investigations have taken has been to employ token reinforcers, such as colored chips or point cards, to improve and maintain improvement of social and/or academic behaviors. Items such as candy, gum, toys, and money have served as backup reinforcers to these tokens, since tokens are exchanged for them.

The problems that can be created, even by an effective token reinforcement system, may be numerous. Not only can token systems be costly in terms of teacher time, but they also may involve an additional burden to already strained school budgets. The administration of tokens such as colored chips, and the overseeing of the exchange of tokens for backup reinforcers such as toys, may be an unfamiliar role for teachers. Also, parents may be given no function in a token system, although it is recognized that parents can play an integral part in an effective program for children with special needs.[6]

These considerations mean that a token system must make a contribution to the amelioration of the children's learning difficulties that is significantly greater than that possible with less costly procedures. As K. D. O'Leary and W. C. Becker have indicated,[7] the rationale usually offered for employing token systems is that other incentives available to the school, such as teacher attention and grades, have not been effective, since the children involved still exhibit a high frequency of asocial and nonacademic behaviors.

The primary goal of the present research was to assess whether a pay-for-grades token reinforcement system could increase academic behavior to levels higher than those achievable with the usually available school incentives. Another aim was to reduce the problems often associated with token systems. By employing grades as tokens, the teacher was not subjected to an unfamiliar role. With weekly allowances as backup reinforcers for grades, parents were able to administer the exchange aspect of the system and were consequently involved in the program. Because parents managed the exchange of tokens for backup reinforcers, and because corrections and some form of grades are an integral part of almost any instructional program, the teacher spent little extra time in the execution of this system. Since the parents of the children of the present study were accustomed to giving their children allowances, neither parents nor school assumed added costs.

Method

Subjects. The subjects were ten students in a learning-disabilities class that was held in Skyline Elementary School, Roesland School District 92, Shawnee Mission, Kansas, during the 1966-1967 school year. This class was one of several special classes operated by the Northeast Johnson County Cooperative Program in Special Education, Johnson County, Kansas.

These ten students, eight boys and two girls, ranged in age from ten to thirteen years and were selected for a learning-disabilities class on the basis that although their ability levels were above the educable mentally retarded range, their achievement levels were retarded by at least two years in one or more academic areas. All students had received medical and/or psychological evaluations that had suggested minimal brain damage with accompanying emotional disturbance. Case histories reported all students to be highly distractible and prone to engage in disruptive behaviors.

Data are reported on eight of the ten students, as data were incomplete on two students who returned to regular classes after the first week of the pay for weekly grades period.

Teacher. Prior to teaching the Skyline special class, the teacher had had five years of full-time teaching and five years of teacher substitute work in grades K-8. She had obtained her M. Ed. in Special Education from the University of Kansas, with the major part of the academic work for this degree involving courses in behavior modification and operant psychology. Her master's thesis dealt with a basic education program for school dropouts that employed a token reinforcement system.[8]

Volunteers from a women's service organization also participated in the program as teacher aides. These aides served mainly to correct and grade the children's academic work.

Classroom. The Skyline special classroom is similar to self-contained classrooms found in many elementary schools. With the exception of desk shields extending about twenty inches above and on three sides of a desk's writing surface, no effort was made to reduce stimuli in the room to a bare minimum, as is sometimes recommended.[9] Decorative curtains served as window drapes; different colors surfaced the walls, floor, and ceiling; books, teaching materials, and art supplies were always in full view. Walls served as display areas for the children's art work and construction projects. The room often had a festive air as the children decorated it for the various seasons.

Instructional Materials and Programing. The commercially available academic materials used were those that might be found in any elementary classroom. Where possible, the children worked on programed instructional materials, such as the SRA reading series (Science Research Associates, Inc.). Otherwise, the children did workbook assignments (Ginn and Company arithmetic workbooks, for example). Such materials were used because they require overt responses.

Prior to the beginning of school and during the first two days of school, the teacher tested the children with the *Durrell Analysis of Reading Difficulty* and the *SRA Achievement Series* tests.[10] On the basis of these measures, children were placed at academic levels in each of the five instructional areas of the class: reading, arithmetic, spelling, penmanship, and English composition and grammar.

Children were given weekly assignments in each of these five instructional areas, with one assignment sheet for each area. Assignment sheets listed the materials to be worked on each day and the total number of responses assigned, and provided space for the child to record his starting and finishing time and for the teacher (or aide) to record daily the number of responses completed, the number correct, and the child's grade. In each academic area, children were required to complete all previous assignments before going on to new work. If any work was not completed by the week's end, it was assigned for the following week as a new assignment.

Observations and Recording Procedures. Children were observed by a research assistant through the one-way mirror of a room adjacent to the classroom. A sound system was arranged so that the assistant could hear what occurred.

Observation time covered the first three hours of every morning: the reading and arithmetic periods, together with a short break between these periods in which the children had physical education or recess. Attending was defined as direct orientation toward work materials; that is, a child was scored as attending if he was sitting at his desk with materials open and before him, and eyes directed toward these materials. Any contact with teacher or aide (raising hand for teacher help or discussion of assignment) was likewise scored as attending. In group work, a child was scored as attending if he was oriented toward work materials, to a reciting fellow student, or to the teacher, or if he himself was responding orally to a lesson. All behaviors other than those specified above were scored as non-attending.

An attending score was obtained for each child once every three minutes. From 90 to 120 seconds were required to observe and score the entire class. The remaining 60 to 90 seconds of the three-minute period were used to note teacher and aide behaviors and prepare for the next group of observations.

The reading period lasted about 80 minutes and the arithmetic 60, so that approximately 26 and 20 measures of attending to reading and arithmetic, respectively, could be made on each child on each school day. A child would at times finish an assignment early; thus, there were fewer observations of that child for that assignment period. The observer stopped recording the behavior of a child when he had turned his materials in to the teacher or aide and these materials had been certified as complete.

Although the observer was aware of the general orientation of the investigation, he was informed neither of the details of the pay-for-grades procedure, nor of when it was put into effect.

Baseline Period. Incentives available in the school were employed as described below.

- Recess. The children earned recess by the successful completion of all of their assignments for the given assignment week up to the point of a given recess period. Children were required to work through recess if their work was not complete.
- Free-Time Activities. When a child had completed all of his assigned work before a given academic period had ended, he was free to go to a free-time table to draw, paint, or construct, or he could read a book of his choice at his seat. Free-time activities were not available to children until all work was complete.
- Special Privileges. School errands were run by those children who were working hard and well, or who had shown recent improvement in the quality of their work. Line leaders and monitors were chosen on the same basis.
- Group versus Individual Lunch. Children who had all of their work complete by lunchtime earned the privilege of eating in the school cafeteria with the rest of the school. Those whose work was incomplete ate at their desks, in silence.
- Teacher Attention. The attention of the teacher was contingent upon appropriate working behaviors of the children. For

example, the teacher would say to a hard-working child, "Good for you, you're working well, and that's the way you'll become smart in arithmetic and return to regular class sooner." Inappropriate behavior was either ignored or, if disruptive, was punished.

• Weekly Grades. Every week children were given grades to take home to their parents. The parents signed the grade sheets, which the children then returned to the teacher. Both daily and weekly grades were included on these grade sheets. *A* grades indicated that a child had finished his work with 90 percent correct, *B* indicated 80 to 90 percent, *C* indicated 79 percent and below, and *Incomplete* indicated that a child had failed to finish his assigned work.

The teacher conducted group parent conferences once a month at the school, during which time the parents were instructed to praise grades of *A* and *B* and to compliment children for their hard work. Grades of *C* were acceptable, while brief expressions of sorrow were to be paired with grades of *Incomplete* (for example, "That's too bad you didn't finish all your work in reading this week"), and children were to be encouraged to finish all work for the next week.

Discussions about academic behaviors and their reinforcers were undertaken by the teacher with individual children as well as with the entire group. These discussions were kept brief and never were held when a child was emotionally upset. Through these discussions it was hoped that the children would gain a further awareness of how they could succeed academically and what rewards would accompany such achievement.

To be maximally effective, reinforcers must be consistently applied. In this case, academic behaviors were consistently reinforced, while nonacademic behaviors were extinguished (not reinforced) or punished (resulting in the removal of some reinforcer). To ensure consistency, both the observer and the first author of this article observed the teacher (and aides, where appropriate) and made at least one report a day to the teacher concerning her application of behavior modification techniques. For example, a tally sheet was kept of the number of times the teacher attended to academic behaviors during the school day and of the number of times she incorrectly attended to inappropriate, nonacademic behaviors. By daily discussion of this tally sheet, the teacher was able to increase her frequency of attending to good behaviors and could virtually ignore the unacceptable ones.

The teacher was likewise informed if a child had earned but had not been awarded the opportunity to run a school errand, and if a child should not have been allowed recess because of incomplete work. With this information feedback, the teacher appeared to increase her behavior modification skills.

Pay for Weekly Grades Period. All procedures employed during the baseline period were continued in identical fashion during the

119

pay period. However, the weekly grades of the baseline period now acquired an additional backup reinforcer: the payment of a weekly allowance to children by their parents on the basis of the children's grades for all subject areas. All the children had received some allowance previous to this period, but the amount received had not depended on their weekly grades. Children were paid for the average weekly grade of each subject area.

At a parent-teacher conference toward the end of the baseline period, parents were instructed in the pay-for-grades procedures. As an example, parents were told that a child might be paid ten cents for *A*'s, five cents for *B*'s, and one cent for *C*'s, while *Incompletes* would lead to a subtraction of the *A* amount, or minus ten cents. The parents determined the precise amounts on the basis of how much money their child was accustomed to having and the cost of the items he would be expected to purchase from his earnings. Amounts actually paid by parents for the weekly grades ranged from the values in the above example up to five times each grade amount in the example. Thus, with the five areas of the special class, plus physical education and music, which the children took with the other children in the school, children's maximum earnings varied from $.70 to $3.50. With *Incompletes* being subtracted from earned allowance, it was possible for a child to owe his parents money. Toward this eventuality, parents were told to allow such an indebted child to perform some household chores over the weekend to square his debt. No money beyond the debt was to be earned, however. One indebted child, during the early part of the pay period, settled the debt by cleaning the garage.

Parents were asked to sit down with their child each Friday afternoon when the child brought home his weekly grades, calculate with the child the amount earned, and then pay him this amount. This was to be made an important weekly event. Parents were also asked to see that a large portion of the allowance be immediately consumed, and that the child be expected to pay with his earnings for all items he valued highly. Such things as movies, sweets, models, dolls, horseback riding, the purchase and care of pets, makeup, and inexpensive clothes were to be the children's financial responsibility. The children were not allowed to earn other money about the home, and any added money that came as presents or that was earned outside the home was to be banked. Such procedures helped to maintain the child's need and desire for money at high levels so that money would continue to serve as an effective reinforcer for academic behavior.

Parents informed their children of the pay procedure on the day before the start of the week that would lead to the first payment for weekly grades. Parents also told their children what items the child would be expected to purchase with his earned allowance.

The pay procedure was continued for the remainder of the year for all children, including children who returned to regular classes.

Regular classroom teachers were instructed to give these children grades of D and F, as well as higher grades, when their work was at these levels. A grade of D subtracted the B amount from a child's allowance, while a grade of F subtracted the A amount. When a child had successfully made the transition to regular class and had performed well for an extended period of time, the length of grade periods was increased (for example, from once a week to once every two weeks, with appropriate increases in amounts paid for grades). In this way, it was hoped to strengthen the child's academic behavior further and to prepare him for the longer grading periods he would encounter in his future schooling.

Results

A marked increase in attending to reading occurred in the pay period compared with the baseline period (see *Figure 1*). Overall medians increased from 68 percent in the baseline period to 86 percent in the pay period.

FIGURE I.
Patterns of Medians in Attending to Reading

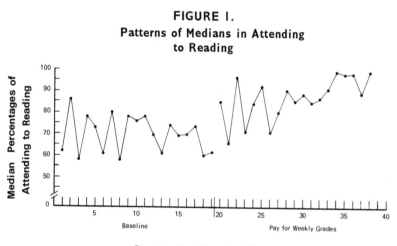

Consecutive Days in Class

It is necessary to be certain that the increases in the pay period cannot be attributed to progressive, though perhaps gradual, increases during the baseline period, since the consequences employed during the baseline period may have been increasing attending. Since the most powerful test for such trends was desired, an analysis of variance, rather than a nonparametric test, was performed on the baseline data, yielding an F ratio of less than one (see *Table 1*), which allows the retention of the hypothesis that the baseline procedures had no tendency to increase attending to reading. By computing eta square, it was estimated that trends accounted for only 6 percent of the variance of the baseline period.

TABLE 1
Analysis of Variance for Baseline Trends
of Percentages of Attending to Reading

Source	SS	df	MS	F
Between Subjects	32345.368	7		
Within Subjects	36351.684	144		
Trends	4337.302	18	240.96	< 1
Residual	32014.382	126	254.08	

The increase in attending to reading from the baseline period to the pay period was significant (see *Table 2*); $p < .005$, one tailed Wilcoxon Matched Pairs Signed Ranks Test.[11] The data for each student conformed very closely to the pattern of medians shown in *Figure 1*. Thus, it can be inferred that the token reinforcement system led to substantial gains in attending to reading for all students.

TABLE 2
Subjects' Median Percentages
of Attending to Reading

Subjects	Baseline	Pay	Increase
S1	71	89	18
S2	82	95	13
S3	23	77	54
S4	83	93	10
S5	72	83	11
S6	72	79	7
S7	75	83	8
S8	62	75	13

Note: Wilcoxon $T = 0$; $p < .005$ (one tailed test)

TABLE 3
Analysis of Variance for Baseline Trends
of Percentages of Attending to Arithmetic

Source	SS	df	MS	F
Between Subjects	36957.158	7		
Within Subjects	51337.684	144		
Trends	7265.842	18	403.678	1.154*
Residual	44071.842	126	349.776	

*$p > .25$

Similar results were obtained in arithmetic (see *Figure 2*). Overall medians increased from 70 percent in the baseline period to 86 percent in the pay period. The analysis of variance for trends during the arithmetic baseline period also yielded an insignificant F ratio (see *Table 3*; $F = 1.154$, $p > .25$). Through eta square, it was estimated that only 8 percent of the baseline arithmetic variance could be accounted for by trends.

FIGURE 2.

Patterns of Medians in Attending
to Arithmetic

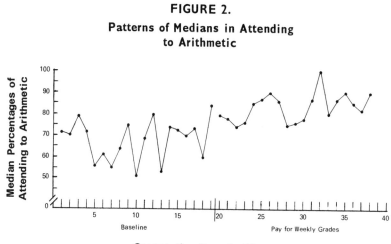

Consecutive Days in Class

Attending to arithmetic also showed significant increases for the pay period over the baseline period (see *Table 4; p < .005*, one tailed Wilcoxon Test). Six subjects' graphs showed the same general form as the median graph in *Figure 2*. Thus, it can be inferred that the token system led to substantial gains in attending to arithmetic for these six subjects. The remaining two subjects (Subjects 2 and 7) showed gradual but steady increases in attending to arithmetic for the last ten days of the baseline period. Consequently, it cannot be concluded that the increases in attending to arithmetic shown by these two subjects for the pay period over the baseline period can be attributed solely to the pay for weekly grades procedure.

TABLE 4

Subjects' Median Percentages
of Attending to Arithmetic

Subjects	Baseline	Pay	Increase
S1	67	88	21
S2	89	94	5
S3	36	79	43
S4	80	94	14
S5	83	88	5
S6	63	76	13
S7	64	81	17
S8	53	68	15

Note: Wilcoxon $T = 0$; $p < .005$ (one tailed test)

Percentages of attending were determined in the following way: if a total of twenty observations were made on a child in arithmetic, and if, of these, ten were scored as attending, the child's percentage of attending to arithmetic on that day was 10/20 x 100 or 50 percent.

Reliability checks were made between the first author and the observer on four occasions, two for reading and two for arithmetic. Reliability coefficients, estimated by the Pearson product moment formula and calculated across subjects with day and academic area held constant, were .91 and .95 for reading and .88 and .90 for arithmetic.

The attending data were obtained during October, November, and part of December, 1966. The month of September was used to refine the observational techniques and to ensure that instructional procedures and materials were adequate to meet each child's needs.

Although the observations were stopped after Christmas vacation, the number of *Incompletes* (with the exception of Subject 8) and the percentages of correct responses indicated that subjects maintained for the remainder of the school year the level of academic behavior attained during the pay period. Students' earnings varied from week to week and ranged from 30 to 85 percent of maximum possible earnings.

As the working efficiency of the students increased, larger assignments were given. At the end of the school year, all ten students were working successfully one to four levels above their starting levels in all academic areas. Six of the ten students were returned full time to regular classes to one grade higher than the ones they had been in during the previous school year. For two of these six, grading periods were extended to four weeks and for one, to two weeks, while the other three remained on the one week period since they were returned to regular classes with only two months of the school year left. In spite of the fact that regular classroom teachers were instructed to give grades of *D* and *F* when appropriate, half of the returned students consistently earned *B* averages and half earned *C* averages. At the close of the school year, all six of the returned students were again promoted, this time by their regular classroom teachers.

Discussion

The present study demonstrated that a token reinforcement system with grades as tokens and allowances as backup reinforcers can significantly increase levels of academic behavior beyond those maintained by the systematic application of other reinforcers available to a school.

All students, with the exception of Subject 8, maintained these increased levels of academic behavior. This subject, with the pay still in effect, would alternate several weeks of complete work and high grades with several weeks of incomplete work. His parents reported that they had never reached agreement on the proper administration of the pay procedures and were, consequently, very inconsistent in its application. The subject was originally required to purchase his weekly movie and a construction model, yet his parents said that they gave him these rewards even when his earnings were insufficient to purchase them. One parent, on several occasions, had claimed all of his earnings as payment for misdemeanors committed at home. In the spring of the year he acquired a high level of social and academic behavior that was maintained for the remainder of the school year. This change in his behavior was coincidental with the death of one of his parents.

Grades have long been the token reinforcement system of schools. But as a reinforcer's effectiveness is directly proportional to its immediacy of presentation,[12] an apparent weakness of this grade system has been that grade reports are presented to children every six to nine weeks, a long delay of reinforcement for a child of elementary school age.

Teachers must correct children's work to ensure learning, and it is but a small step from corrections to grades. Although the teacher of the present study had volunteer aides to assist in the grading, the teacher felt that she could carry out the daily grading and weekly reports, and actually did for the many days that aides were absent.

No test was made to test the effect of the allowance backup reinforcer in the maintenance of high levels of academic behavior for the remainder of the school year. This effect could have been tested by paying the children their allowances independently of their weekly grades. If attending to academic materials had decreased significantly with this change, evidence would have been provided for a maintaining effect for this backup reinforcer. The risk of returning students to their less efficient levels of the baseline period overruled the possible gains in scientific information, and this analysis was not made.

Conclusion

The token reinforcement system used in the present study increased levels of academic behavior with highly distractible and disruptive children. Several additional advantages are inherent in this token system. First, teachers need not spend valuable time in overseeing the exchange of tokens for backup reinforcers. Parents can manage this task at home. Secondly, parents are frequently able to bear the cost of the allowance backup reinforcer, as many parents provide allowances for their children anyway. For parents unable to bear this cost, it seems likely that a service organization could be found that would contribute funds that parents could then pay to their children on the basis of weekly grades. Finally, the present system can open, as it did in this case, an effective channel of communication and cooperation between parents and teachers of children with special educational needs.

NOTES

1. D. Bushell, P. A. Wrobel, and M. L. McCloskey, "Some Effects of Normative Reinforcement on Classroom Study Behavior." Unpublished manuscript, Webster College, St. Louis, Missouri, 1967.

2. M. Clark, J. Lackowicz, and M. Wolf, "A Pilot Basic Education Program for School Dropouts Incorporating a Token Reinforcement System," *Behavior Research and Therapy*, 6, No. 2 (1968).

3. K. D. O'Leary and W. C. Becker, "Behavior Modification of an Adjustment Class: A Token Reinforcement System," *Exceptional Children*, 33 (1967), 637-642.

4. M. M. Wolf, D. K. Giles, and V. R. Hall, "Experiments with Token Reinforcement in a Remedial Classroom," *Behavior Research and Therapy*, 6 (1968), 51-64.

5. R. C. Anderson, "Educational Psychology," *Annual Review of Psychology*, ed. P. R. Farnsworth, Vol. 18 (Palo Alto, Calif.: Annual Reviews, 1967), pp. 129-164; R. J. Whelan, "The Relevance of Behavior Modification Procedures for Teachers of Emotionally Disturbed Children," *Intervention Approaches in Educating Emotionally Disturbed Children*, ed. P. Knoblock (New York, N.Y.: Syracuse University Press, 1966), pp. 35-78.

6. W. M. Cruickshank, *The Brain-Injured Child in Home, School, and Community* (Syracuse, N.Y.: Syracuse University Press, 1967).

7. O'Leary and Becker, "Behavior Modification of an Adjustment Class."

8. Clark, Lackowicz, and Wolf, "A Pilot Basic Education Program."

9. Cruickshank, *The Brain-Injured Child*.

10. Donald D. Durrell, *Durrell Analysis of Reading Difficulty* (New York, N.Y.: Harcourt, Brace & World, 1955); L. B. Thorpe, D. W. Lefever, and R. A. Naslund, *SRA Achievement Series* (Chicago, Ill.: Science Research Associates, Inc., 1954-58).

11. S. Siegel, *Nonparametric Statistics*, (New York, N.Y.: McGraw-Hill, 1956).

12. S. W. Bijou and D. M. Baer, *Child Development*, Vol. 1 (New York, N.Y.: Appleton-Century-Crofts, 1961).

Chapter 2

The Learning Center Concept

Frank M. Hewett
Frank D. Taylor
Alfred A. Artuso
Herbert C. Quay

PAST AND PRESENT efforts to evaluate, classify, describe, and provide educational programs for exceptional children are being seriously questioned by many in the field of education. The specialized, self-contained classes that have evolved for handicapped students, the degree of specialization found in graduate courses, state credential requirements, and public school financing may be operating to the detriment of the students we are ostensibly seeking to help.[1] Questions about the possible limited effectiveness of special education curriculum and instructional techniques, and doubts about cost effectiveness, along with more profound doubts about the social-psychological impact of the traditional special classes have increased.[2] A recent survey of fifty-seven special education researchers, conducted by The Council for Exceptional Children Information Center, identified behavior modification, alternatives to traditional disability groupings, and special class placement as the principal current issues in the field of special education.[3]

Many parents, as well as educators, question the desirability of traditional self-contained classrooms for many exceptional children. Labeling, damage to self-concept, compartmentalization, concerns by minority groups, and loss of stimulating opportunities, as well as questions about the constitutionality of some current testing and grouping practices, are matters of increasing concern. Furthermore, some school districts are unable to offer a full range of programs for handicapped students because of the demand for special classes, each with its own specially trained teacher.

The decade of the seventies will certainly be marked by the search for, and widespread adoption of, new methods of instruction and new models for service delivery. The emphasis may well shift from the medico-psychological model to educational models whose philosophical and empirical foundations lend themselves to objective, measurable results that can be combined with an opportunity to evaluate cost-effectiveness.

The authors share two basic premises about exceptional children. The first belief is that all exceptional children are first and foremost learners: learners who have often been labeled and placed in separate self-contained rooms because of handicaps. The second belief is that it is desirable to remove as many exceptional children as possible from separate self-contained rooms and integrate them for optimum periods of time in regular classrooms. This assumes, of course, that the exceptional children are prepared for and supported during the time they are in the regular classroom.

W ITH THESE two philosophical premises in mind, and as an outgrowth of an earlier program, which was based on an engineered classroom concept of behavior modification,[4] the authors began to conceptualize The Madison School Plan. It was conceived as an operational learning center that would facilitate the grouping of students according to their learning deficits as opposed to traditional grouping by exceptionality and/or diagnostic categories.[5]

Students are often tested, classified, and grouped according to how well they perform or rate on a variety of measures that evaluate such factors as vision, hearing, motor coordination, intelligence, and perceptual ability. If a child scores from 88 to 112 on the intelligence scale or continuum, he is rated "average or normal" and is placed in the regular classroom. If another child scores significantly higher or above 132 on the intelligence continuum, he may be classified "gifted" and be given "enrichment opportunities." Still another child may score below 70 and be placed in a special classroom for the educable mentally retarded (EMR). In the special classroom for the educable mentally retarded, he will be seen as a different kind of student, taught in a different way, with different expectations, and, sadly enough, he will often become different. The same can be true of students who have auditory, visual, motoric, physical, or perceptual handicaps.

With these facts in mind, the authors were confronted with the task of organizing an educational program, with instructional settings for several traditional disability categories, into one learning center that could serve a typical elementary school. It was decided that one scale or dimension that is common to all children, regardless of possible handicaps, is their readiness for regular classroom functioning.

This common dimension seemed to encompass four basic behaviors or abilities that all children must have in order to succeed in school.

- The first set of behaviors include the ability to pay attention, respond, and follow directions as formulated in a developmental sequence that was discussed elsewhere by the first author.[6] In The Madison School Plan, this has been expanded to include the additional pre-academic skills of taking part verbally or orally and doing what one is told in terms of reasonable class limits. These skills are basic to succeeding in a regular classroom, regardless of the student's visual, intellectual, or physical abilities.

- The second set of behaviors includes the academic abilities of being neat, being correct, being able to read, spell, write, and do arithmetic.

- The third set of behaviors require that the child must be able to function in the instructional settings that occur in the regular classroom: when the teacher is giving directions from the front of the room, when the child is working in a small group, or when the child is working independently. Differing kinds of concentration or attention are required when the entire class is reading silently for information than when the teacher is explaining a new concept at the chalkboard.

- The fourth area is related to the student's susceptibility to regular classroom rewards or reinforcers. While some children are motivated by report card grades, others are encouraged by a smile or word of praise from the teacher, and a few may respond better, at least initially, when given a piece of candy, tokens, or checkmarks that can be exchanged for a small prize.

The authors felt that an instructional program, encompassing the above concepts in a learning center environment, would offer optimum opportunities for children to learn the skills necessary to facilitate maximum regular classroom integration. The operational model, identified as The Madison School Plan, was initiated in September of 1968. It provided an instructional program for exceptional children, based on their specific learning strengths or weaknesses rather than traditional categories for the handicapped. These efforts were made possible through a California State Department of Education Title VI-B Grant.

THE PROJECT was directed toward the demonstration and evaluation of a plan for the education of a group of handicapped children who would have been labeled educable mentally retarded, emotionally disturbed, learning disabled, and visually or auditorily impaired. This plan, to be described in detail below, provides for the education of these children in a setting that allows free flow of children between the regular classes and the specialized facility (learning center). It permits the elimination of traditional disability grouping for all but administrative purposes, and it provides an instructional program that is linked to a continuous assessment of those educational variables that have hindered the performance of the exceptional child in the regular classroom in the past.

The grouping framework utilized in The Madison School Plan was organized by creating four points along the dimension of readiness for regular classroom functioning: Pre-Academic I, Pre-Academic II, Academic I, and Academic II (the regular classroom). Each of these sections in the learning center sets an expectancy according to the four areas of behavior that were mentioned above.

Pre-Academic I

This section of the learning center was conceived as a largely self-contained class grouping of six to twelve students and is essentially an engineered classroom.[7] The strongest instructional setting, teacher-child, or child-independent, is used since students in this section need to learn to sit still, pay attention, respond appropriately, take turns, follow simple directions, get along with others, and begin to develop the ability to function in small groups (*Figure 1*). While the emphasis is on the pre-academic skills discussed above in the first set of behaviors, academic written exercises in reading, spelling, handwriting, and arithmetic, represent the major experiences during the day. It is while working on these academic materials that the students learn to ask for help and finish a task. All of these behaviors are appropriately rewarded. Many of the open-ended, multilevel tasks in use were developed or evaluated by the teachers in the original engineered classroom project and are now commercially available.[8] The highest level of reinforcement for each student is used. This is a continuation of the checkmark system, backed up with candy, food, free time, or a free chance, which is patterned after the Monopoly Game's "Take A Chance" card.

Pre-Academic I is a launching experience in this learning center concept in much the same manner as the engineered classroom was originally intended. The students do not spend any time in the regular classroom. The visually and auditorily impaired, as well as the mentally retarded or emotionally disturbed students who need to master the pre-academic skills necessary to function in the regular classroom, would start in this section of the center. They are children who need the experience of the Pre-Academic I learning environment. The environment is labeled, not the student, and in this way we attempt to avoid the negative effects that sometimes occur with student labels.

Pre-Academic II

At this level the emphasis shifts from pre-academic skills to academic skills. However, the big shift is in the kind of work setting. In Pre-Academic I the children work individually at self-contained units with a teacher or aide. Little or no group work or interaction occurs. In Pre-Academic II, six to eight children sit at a

FIGURE 1

Two Typical Learning Center Classrooms with Connecting Door

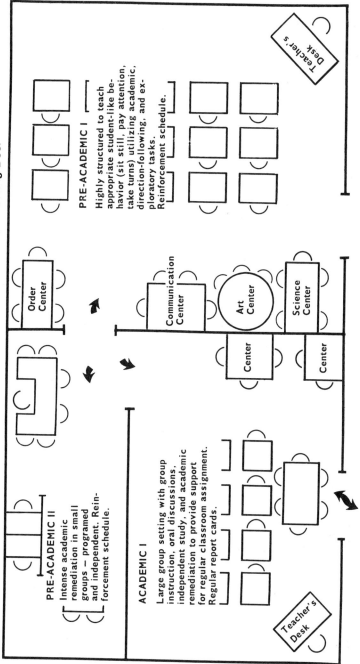

PRE-ACADEMIC I

Highly structured to teach appropriate student-like behavior (sit still, pay attention, take turns) utilizing academic, direction-following, and exploratory tasks. Reinforcement schedule.

Order Center

Communication Center

Art Center

Science Center

Center

Center

Teacher's Desk

PRE-ACADEMIC II

Intense academic remediation in small groups — programed and independent. Reinforcement schedule.

ACADEMIC I

Large group setting with group instruction, oral discussions, independent study, and academic remediation to provide support for regular classroom assignment. Regular report cards.

Teacher's Desk

cluster of tables, getting all of their instruction from the teacher who is in the middle of the cluster. The children work together, cooperate, and are paired off, raising their hands and being encouraged to participate verbally. This section is designed to foster social interaction and verbal participation in group lessons, which was missing in the original engineered classroom design. In terms of reinforcement, the checkmark system is still used, but students are usually limited to trading their completed Work Record Cards for fifteen to twenty minutes of free time. Beginning with Pre-Academic II, each student is integrated into a regular classroom for at least a few minutes during the day.

Academic I

This section of the learning center is a simulated regular classroom setting for twelve to twenty-five children who have primary academic problems that can be dealt with in a large teacher-class setting. These students have the ability to spend increasing amounts of time in the regular classroom and have a readiness for the more traditional system of grading in terms of effort, quality of work, and citizenship. In this setting, the teacher leads class discussions and presents lessons to the large group in reading, arithmetic, spelling, social studies, and English. Students are grouped within this setting in the same manner expected by a regular classroom teacher, and opportunities for silent, independent study are also present. Emphasis is placed on helping each student with the specific skills needed to increase the amount of time spent in a regular classroom.

Academic II

This is the regular classroom in the school, with twenty-eight to thirty-five students, and it follows the typical public school program. All handicapped students in the program are assigned to one of the Pre-Academic I, Pre-Academic II, or Academic I settings. Those in the latter two groups are integrated for varying periods of time in Academic II.

T HE EXISTING six elementary and two secondary learning centers are located in regular public schools in Santa Monica, California. They serve the exceptional students as well as selected regular students in the individual schools where they are located. Transportation of students is held to a minimum since the problems of having separate self-contained classrooms for each area of exceptionality have been dramatically reduced.

Students with auditory or visual handicaps are assigned to an appropriate setting within the center and are integrated into regular classrooms for varying lengths of time, depending on their abilities. These students as well as other students in the center have the services of specialists in oral communications, lip reading, braille, mobility instruction, and speech therapy. It is not unusual to see several mentally retarded or visually impaired children profiting from participation in an oral communication lesson that is designed primarily for the hearing handicapped. The same might be true for lessons in mobility or speech articulation.

Usually two classrooms that are next to each other, with or without a door between them, are converted into a center. It is important to keep in mind the needs of the students to be served and the composition of the groups before arbitrarily setting up the rooms within the center. It has been found that although the room arrangement described in *Figure 1* is generally in use in the operational centers in Santa Monica, there must be flexibility. Several other variations have been utilized when the particular needs of the students in any one school require different instructional emphasis *(Figure 2)*.

A daily schedule for the three settings within the learning center is carefully planned to provide individual, independent, and group lessons that relate to specific student needs. Commercially available materials are utilized, programed instructional techniques employed, and teacher preparation time is kept to a minimum *(Figure 3)*.

The model implies, in essence, that first you assign children to a grouping category based on the initial work-up, and once this assignment has been made, you zero in on a continual detailed assessment over a period of time, rather than stop with just an initial full-scale preplacement assessment, which is often the case in traditional programs.

In order to maintain a continuous assessment of each child's progress and provide data for reassignment to different groupings, two types of procedures are utilized: a checkmark system in Pre-Academic I and II, and a numerical rating system in Academic I and II. In the checkmark system, the teacher gives each child a maximum of ten checkmarks, in the form of alphabet letters that represent attending to work, following directions, etc., every twenty minutes during the morning.

This system makes it possible to determine the percentage of rating points earned by each student over the week in relation to his readiness for regular class functioning, as well as a profile of pre-academic or academic areas in which he needs to improve. In the Academic I numerical rating system, the teacher gives each student a one-to-five rating in the areas of quality of work and citizenship, each hour. Weekly percentages reflect the child's functioning in these traditional grading areas. Each regular classroom teacher who has contact with a project child also is asked to provide a weekly rating in these areas for each child. When considering reassignment for a given child, his progress, or lack of it, as shown in the assessment data, is carefully reviewed.

At the beginning of the school year, as many of the educationally handicapped children with learning disabilities as possible are assigned to regular classrooms. As students are referred out to the special program because they cannot handle the behavioral and aca-

FIGURE 2

Variations of the Learning Center Classroom Model

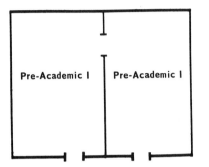

All of the students need to learn how to sit still, follow directions, take turns, and raise their hands. As some students progress, they will move into the Pre-Academic II and Academic I portion of the center, which will evolve as one of the Pre-Academic I settings is converted. This is the most widely used variation when starting a new center and may be the best starting model.

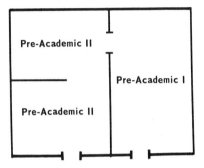

Some of the students are beyond Pre-Academic I and can function in Pre-Academic II settings, but are not ready for Academic I. This will evolve later as one Pre-Academic II setting is converted into an Academic I.

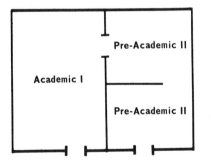

None of the children in this model need the experiences of Pre-Academic I since they can all follow directions, raise their hands, and take turns.

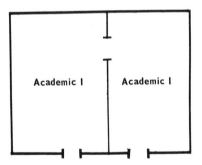

All of the children can be integrated into regular classrooms during the day and only need occasional supportive instructional assistance.

FIGURE 3
Daily Schedule of Activities in the Learning Center

Time	Academic I	Pre-Academic II	Pre-Academic I
8:45 9:00	Typical Class Opening Exercises		Direction-following Task
9:00	*(Reading)* Typical large class reading program. Group and individual reading. Basal Readers, SRA, etc.	*(Reading)* Remedial-reading instruction or motivation for story writing — Story writing or remedial follow-up task — Word study. Individual reading, programed material	*(Reading)* Individual Reading — Word Study — Skill Reading
10:00	........Recess .... Recess .... Recess ....
10:15	*(Arithmetic)* Typical large class program. Discussions. Group and independent work	*(Arithmetic)* Arithmetic instruction. Specific follow-up tasks. Remedial opportunities	*(Arithmetic)* Arithmetic Drill — Instruction — Follow-Up
10:55	Spelling	Language Development and/or Spelling	Language Skills
11:25	............Lunch ....Lunch .... Lunch ....
12:25 12:40	Read to Class — Social Studies English Art	Pre-Academic II students join ←—either—→ group according to their individual needs	*(Exploratory)* Art Science Order Communication
1:50	........Recess .... Recess .... Recess ....
2:00	Physical Education		Opportunities for individualized remedial instruction
2:30	Individual Tutoring		
3:00			

demic demands of the class, an attempt is made to preserve some link with the regular class by having the child return for morning exercises, P. E., music, etc. As they demonstrate academic and/or behavioral improvement, an effort is made to increase their time in the regular class until optimum placement is reached. The evaluation procedures aid in determining this reassignment. The EMR children start in the special program, but early in the school year efforts are made to establish a regular classroom link for them. During the year their progress on the evaluation ratings is noted and integration increased whenever possible.

THE AUTHORS are aware that any attempt to overhaul practices in special education has to take two things into account. *First,* you have to be able to demonstrate that what you're doing has more in it for the exceptional child than what was being done before. You're accountable to show that this child is indeed better off in Pre-Academic I or II than he was in the EMR or EH class. If you can't do that, you're going to a lot of trouble for no purpose at all. The *second* thing you have to do is answer the questions of practicality and ease of replication. If your program costs two or three times as much as existing programs, and if it requires more teachers and additional facilities, it's probably not going to be replicated very many places. The child has to be given something more than he is given in the traditional framework, and the field of special education should not be encumbered with costs beyond any reasonable level.

In summary, The Madison School Plan, developed over a three-year period, attempts to combine traditional categories of exceptionality along a dimension of readiness for regular classroom functioning and provide education for exceptional children in Pre-Academic I, Pre-Academic II, and Academic I groupings. Assessment and evaluation of the children is based on academic and behavioral functioning, and a major goal of the plan is to increase the amount of time the exceptional child participates in a regular classroom program.

NOTES

1. L. M. Dunn, "Special Education for the Mildly Retarded — Is Much of it Justifiable?", *Exceptional Children,* 35 (1968), 5-22.

2. M. S. Lilly, "Special Education: A Teapot in a Tempest," *Exceptional Children,* 37 (1970), 43-48; L. Blackman, "The Dimensions of a Science of Special Education," *Mental Retardation,* 5 (1967), 7-11; L. Connor, "The Heart of the Matter," *Exceptional Children,* 34 (1968), 579; H. C. Quay, "The Facets of Educational Exceptionality: A Conceptual Framework for Assessment, Grouping and Instruction," *Exceptional Children,* 35 (1968), 25.

3. J. B. Jordan, "The Now Way to Know," *Education and Training of the Mentally Retarded* (February 1971), 29-41.

4. F. M. Hewett, "Educational Engineering with Emotionally Disturbed Children," *Exceptional Children* (March 1967), 459-467.

5. M. M. Soloway, "A Descriptive Study of the Madison School Plan." Unpublished master's thesis (Los Angeles, Calif.: University of California, 1970).

6. F. M. Hewett, "A Hierarchy of Educational Tasks for Children with Learning Disorders," *Exceptional Children*, 31 (1964), 207-214.

7. R. J. Stillwell et al., "An Educational Solution," *Focus on Exceptional Children*, 2, No. 1 (March 1970), 1-15.

8. F. D. Taylor, A. A. Artuso, and F. M. Hewett, *Creative Art Tasks for Children*; idem, *Individualized Reading Skills Improvement*; idem, *Individualized Arithmetic Instruction* (Denver, Colo.: Love Publishing Company, 1970).

Chapter 3

Behavioral Modification
in a Junior High
Learning Disabilities Classroom

Patricia A. Nolen
Harold P. Kunzelmann
Norris G. Haring

Reprinted by permission of the authors and *Exceptional Children*, November 1967

NEW EVIDENCE supporting behavioral modification techniques in special education classrooms is reported almost monthly. Those who have extended operant behavioral principles to classroom learning have suggested that complex academic response repertoires may be amenable to a methodology based on a functional analysis of behavior.[1] Whether or not this approach can be applied to situations beyond the short-term clinical or tutorial periods, however, has been the basis for continuing doubt. The heterogeneous enrollments and complex curriculum requirements in most regularly scheduled classrooms have seemed to limit the functionality of operant behavioral analysis to appropriate social behaviors or to short sequences of the program. Preliminary findings from the classrooms of the University of Washington Experimental Education Unit, however, have suggested otherwise. Here ongoing investigations seem to indicate that any limitations imposed upon behavioral analysis at the outset may be premature.[2]

The Experimental Education Unit was organized to provide for the study, assessment, and remediation of educational retardation. Because its research responsibilities are diverse, and because it provides services for teacher training as well as services for exceptional children, the behavioral deviancies of its children span a wider range than is found within the usual special education classrooms. Diagnostic categories represented within any one class are further differentiated as a result of the school unit's involvement in the multidisciplinary Mental Retardation and Child Development Center. Despite the multiplicity and heterogeneity of learning problems, however, each of the unit's five classrooms has provided sufficient evidence in one school term to warrant further investigation of functional behavioral analysis as a classroom teaching and management technique.

The data reported here were taken from the junior high classroom during its first year of operation. Students enrolled in this class were twelve to sixteen years in age, with individual achievement levels ranging from preschool to sixth grade. Diagnostic categories and recorded behavioral deviancies covered as wide a span for the one grouping as did the achievement levels. On the referrals, students were listed as "passive-aggressive," "psychotic," "dyslexic," "aphasic," having "generalized mental retardation," being "emotionally disturbed," or "neurologically impaired," together with a generally pessimistic prognosis for any long term effect of remedial teaching. Such classifications are not used as criteria for the school unit's enrollment; demonstrated learning deficits are the preferred criteria. With these deficits as primary concerns, the educational diagnostician seeks to identify deficiencies the child may have in content or extent and/or rate of learning within any one or a number of specific academic or social behavioral skill areas. This diagnosis by skill specifics, rather than by physical or psychological deficit, is considered fundamental to the application of behavioral management techniques in the unit's classrooms. It has allowed a much broader view of remedial teaching, which, contrary to the popular notion, has not seemed to neglect the web of dynamic interrelationships posed by such factors as "motivation" or "inadequate self concept." Although these factors have been included within the teaching context, they have been considered as "the ability to respond successfully and effectively." By standards of skill specifics, then, the frequency of accurate academic responses is of primary consideration here.

Initial organization of the classroom entailed an extensive tabulation and compilation of all skills that could be identified within any one academic area. Standard test achievement levels such as "third grade reading comprehension" or "first grade computational ability" simply did not supply the teacher with the precise information on which remediation as behavioral modification could be based. In place of the broad summarization of standardized tests, behavioral definitions of skill sequences were abstracted largely from programed academic curricula for which adequate developmental and field testing data were available. Eventually this detailed outline was expanded to include both teacher designed steps and an increased number of contingencies advocated for optimal learning.[3] An interesting outcome of the analysis was the finding that, for most learners, an optimal program requires less of the former and more of the latter.

It is not new to note that present knowledge allows only an approximation of the structure of any one content area. Within these limitations, an attempt was made to define as many steps in a particular learning sequence as could be identified. It is believed that this may be necessary before attempting to order classroom learning situations for the employment of behavioral modification techniques.

Observers invariably made remarks about the lengthy and detailed skill sequence sheets,[4] saying that although the idea was praiseworthy, a teacher could not possibly know every child's attainment or exact direction of skills at any one time. Those who had the opportunity to test this assumption, however, found that the unit's teachers did in fact know a child's skills and would use and often revise these skill outlines. In the junior high class, for example, a student was not merely "working on multiplication," he was working with multiplication of whole numbers defined in terms of repeated addition or reconstructing multiplication equations with a missing product or missing factor in combinations through 5 x 9 or studying in another area which had been analyzed with similar detail. Answers also referred to comparative rates of performance, computed not between students but between any two performances of the same student.

Program Stimuli

Once both skill sequences and the student's functioning at some point in the sequence were identified, the designation of the program was no simple task of matching student and workbook at some certain grade level. On the contrary, completely individual programs were organized. These were built largely from commercially programed materials together with selections from traditional texts and workbooks. Often the linear progression was achieved only with the design of supplements programed to overcome deficits in the sequence. During the second year of operation, while refinements in programing continued, individualization of instruction for a student became less of a problem than individualization of a particular content area. From these initial programs, preliminary task analyses of specific and generic teaching points were outlined in terms of their distribution and interrelation.

Reinforcement Contingencies

Although the stimulus program (an attempt to define and arrange academic responses) played an important role in the organization of an operant classroom, reinforcement contingencies were the major concern. Two principles guided the exploration of reinforcement contingencies in the unit's classrooms: the first, what is known as "high probability behavior," is a concept well substantiated by the work of D. Premack[5] and L. Homme et al.[6] This behavior occurs at a high rate prior to educational or clinical intervention; it consists of those things the student most often chooses to do, providing a source for "natural" consequences for the manipulation and acceleration of low probability behavior; the second requirement was that both high probability behavior and any other consequences assumed to be "secondary reinforcers" were ultimately acceptable in a traditionally organized classroom. This second principle precluded at the outset the use of money, candy, or trinkets, the "consumable/manipulatable" classifications of the laboratories.[7] Further, the singular use of social approval as a durable reinforcing consequence did not seem to offer the initial control needed for programing the multiple contingencies of a group situation. Moreover, it did not seem that classroom management could be optimally based on the assumption that social approval was a reinforcer for those adolescents with a history of school and interpersonal failure.[8]

In an attempt to standardize the number of stimuli presupposed to be "natural" consequences of high strength behavior, the teacher allotted points for the child's successful completion of each of a number of gradually lengthening academic tasks. A running record of these points was kept at each child's desk, and these points were negotiable at any time for play periods analogous to school recesses or for a variety of enrichment or practical studies in the public schools.[9] The junior high students' most preferred choices for contingent high strength behavior centered on handicrafts, typing, woodworking, organized games, or science units. These choices were somewhat surprising to the teaching staff, who had made an effort to supply what are considered culturally determined "reinforcers" for adolescents by extending the available consequences to include slot cars, models, popular recordings, and teen magazines, on the assumption that such choices would be replaced only by gradually shaping preferences for the more traditional school activities.

Data Collection

Unlike procedures used in the majority of operant studies, the experimenter-teacher did not have the exclusive function of establishing individual behavioral baselines. Using service as one of the operational criteria, baseline or "operant level" was determined by (a) anecdotal records and achievement test scores from the student's school records prior to enrollment in the unit, and (b) rate of daily academic responses recorded on the first day of enrollment. It seemed advisable to begin the teaching method on the first day, with concomitant manipulation of high and low strength behaviors not only from a first day service viewpoint but also due to the ease of its application to a group admitting new members during the school year. The data were recorded in terms of both subject matters and total academic responses for each student over a period of 100 days.

Indications

The resulting data from the first year's efforts at organizing a special education classroom on a behavioral basis are shown in *Figure 1*. These records include only reading and arithmetic responses, excepting the modification of social behaviors which ac-

companied remedial skill instruction. Throughout the twenty-four
week instructional period, an effort was made to define "academic
response" individually for each student and for each particular subject area. In the initial stages of reading, for example, the correct
association of a letter shape with a sound was an adequate response

FIGURE I. Cumulative Academic Record

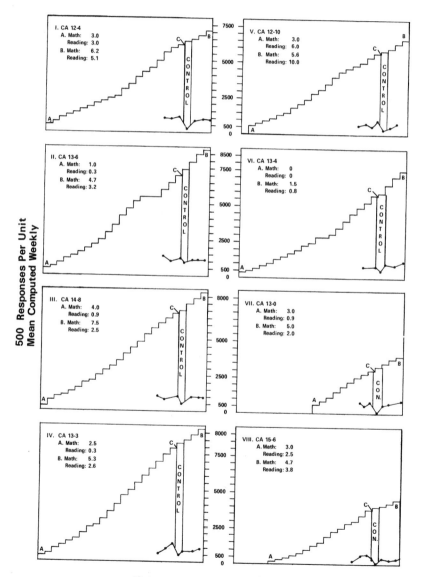

24 Week Instructional Period

for the application of negotiable consequences. Later, however, once the association had been cued, prompted, and practiced without prompts, the single element became part of a chain included in the definition of a succeeding response. In other words, sound-symbol relationships, phonic blending and sight words, and eventually oral reading of a complete sentence were all progressively defined as a single response for recording purposes and for consequence application.

In like manner, arithmetical functioning was ordered in successive stages which began with the manipulation of actual concrete physical quantities, followed by the manipulation of physical representations, then abstract representations prior to any association of numerals with numbers or symbols with operations. As in reading, antecedent steps in any arithmetical sequence were considered chained in subsequent, more complex responses.

Each graph in *Figure 1* represents one student's weekly cumulative record of frequency of correct academic responses in reading and mathematics during that part of the instructional period in which he was enrolled. After a high rate of responding had been established, the procedure was altered in an attempt to isolate the function of contingent delivery of the points negotiable for high strength activities. During this control period, four time allotments for high strength activities were scheduled daily for each student. Unlike the organization of the school day prior and subsequent to the control period, the high strength activities at this time were contingent neither upon accuracy nor on rate of responding. In this way, the free time followed not as a consequence upon completion of work but upon mere passage of time. Point C on each record identifies the cumulative responses during this interval of reversal. A graph of the drop in the mean number of responses during the five day control period and the subsequent rise during reinstatement of contingencies is displayed at the base of each record.

Notations accompanying response records of eight of the junior high students show beginning achievement levels on the basis of referral reports (A), and achievement levels at the close of the first instructional period of approximately 100 days (B). Even though the programs were based largely on a structural linguistic approach in reading and the "new" mathematics process in arithmetic, terminal levels have been determined on the basis of scores on the *Metropolitan Achievement Tests*,[10] an instrument which does not always reflect the newer instructional emphasis on process as well as product.

While the original records note any absences from the classroom during the school day as a result of illness, clinic visits, or scheduled appointments with any of the unit's supporting services, no compensations for resulting discrepancies in response frequencies have been included. Nor do these records show one of the most welcome by-products of the use of high strength activities to reinforce a low entering level of responding. Seldom if ever did observers to the classroom fail to note the personal pride in achievement evidenced verbally by students. Surprisingly, this came not only as a result of a more generous allotment for minimal functioning in a new skill sequence, but also for the gradual reduction in allotment of points for review work of an increasingly complex and time consuming nature.

Not included in this report is a study of the modification of inappropriate classroom social behavior as the primary goal for a thirteen-year-old male prior to an analysis of subject matter functioning. Whereas this particular student was withdrawn by parental request, it must also be noted that his reinstatement was requested by the parent within a short time.

Conclusion

The acceleration of academic response rates of adolescent students with learning disorders participating in this limited application of functional behavioral analysis to academic performance has stimulated wide interest among personnel in surrounding school districts. Reports indicate that similar behavioral management techniques are either under consideration or in practice at this time. Followup studies of three of the students who have been transferred from this classroom show that, although the acceleration of their rates to peaks of 500 or more responses per day have not been maintained under traditional classroom contingency arrangements, in each case levels of achievement have been maintained and response rates have exceeded those of other members of the transfer classrooms. For those students who were maintained for a second teaching session at the unit, a nine week summer vacation did not interrupt the individual response patterns or rates of acceleration.

In addition, the records from the junior high teacher's parental conferences show that there have been changes in the verbal content of the conferences which have accompanied the increases in individual response rates. The most consistent change recorded is a decrease in parental requests for such conferences on the basis of a student's functioning and an increase in parental requests for detailed explanations of the techniques of classroom management. As a result of such parental demands, study groups for parental education have been planned for those parents asking to participate. A decrease in parental requests for conferences concerning academic progress, and an increase in their requests for management information, seem to indicate that the behavioral changes of the students are, in fact, generalizing to situations other than the controlled environment of the classroom.

NOTES

1. S. W. Bijou and P. T. Sturges, "Positive Reinforcers for Experimental Studies with Children — Consumables and Manipulables," *Child Development*, 30 (1958), 151-170; J. S. Birnbrauer et al., "Programmed Instruction

in the Classroom," *Case Studies in Behavior Modification*, eds. L. P. Ullman and L. Krasner (New York, N.Y.: Holt, Rinehart and Winston, 1966), pp. 358-366; A. Staats et al., "Reinforcement Variables in the Control of Unit Reading Response," *Journal of the Experimental Analysis of Behavior*, 7 (1964), 139-149; O. R. Lindsley, "Direct Measurement and Prosthesis of Retarded Behavior," *Journal of Education*, 147 (1964), 62-81; Sister Carolyn Whitlock, "Note on Reading Acquisition: an Extension of Laboratory Principles," *Journal of Experimental Child Psychology*, 3 (1966), 83-85.

2. N. G. Haring and H. P. Kunzelmann, "Finer Focus of Therapeutic Behavior Management," *Educational Therapy*, ed. J. Hellmuth (Seattle, Wash.: Special Child Publications, 1966), pp. 225-251; N. G. Haring and T. C. Lovitt, "Operant Methodology and Educational Technology in Special Education," *Methods in Special Education*, eds. N. G. Haring and R. L. Schiefulbusch (New York, N.Y.: McGraw-Hill, 1967), pp. 12-48.

3. L. Homme et al., "Use of the Premack Principle in Controlling the Behavior of Nursery School Children," *Journal of the Experimental Analysis of Behavior*, 6 (1963), 544.

4. University of Washington College of Education, *Experimental Education Unit Mathematics Skill Sequence Sheet*, Seattle, Washington, 1966.

5. D. Premack, "Reinforcement Theory," *Nebraska Symposium on Motivation*, ed. D. Levine (Lincoln, Nebr.: University of Nebraska Press, 1965), pp. 123-189.

6. Homme et al., "Use of the Premack Principle."

7. Bijou and Sturges, "Positive Reinforcers."

8. S. W. Bijou and D. M. Baer, "Operant Methods in Child Behavior and Development," *Operant Behavior*, ed. W. K. Honig (New York, N.Y.: Appleton-Century-Crofts, 1966) pp. 778-782.

9. Haring and Kunzelmann, "Finer Focus of Therapeutic Behavior Management."

10. W. N. Durost et al., *Metropolitan Achievement Tests* (New York, N.Y.: Harcourt, Brace & World, 1931-1964).

Chapter 4

Precision Teaching
the Learning-Disabled Child

Robert H. Bradfield
Jane Criner

DURING THE PAST two to three decades, debate has flourished, sometimes heatedly, sometimes quietly, with regard to the etiological basis of that which is called *learning disability*. Two main distinctions have emerged from this debate. One is that neurological dysfunction appears to be the cause of learning disabilities, and the other is that such disabilities appear to be emotional in origin. This differentiation is illustrated by the fact that the U.S. Department of Health, Education, and Welfare funds separate teacher-training programs: one for teachers of emotionally disturbed children, and another for teachers of children with learning disabilities. As a result, the term *learning disabilities* has, over time, become more identified with neurological dysfunction.

It is not our intention to become involved in such debate, nor to tilt imaginary windmills, but rather to suggest that whatever the cause, a common denominator does exist between these groups: the behavior of the child. Whatever the original cause, we suggest that the bulk of those behaviors that can be observed in any child, learning disabled or not, can be explained by the laws of learning and can be altered by the systematic application of these same laws.

Operant theory suggests that when meaningful and appropriate stimuli are presented in optimal increments, the desired response should take place, and if that response is followed by a meaningful consequence, the probability is increased that the behavior or response will occur again. In educational terms, this means that when a meaningful and appropriate curriculum is presented to the child in understandable, sequential steps, and he is adequately rewarded for responding correctly to those steps, learning will take place. This will be true whether the learning involves reading a sentence or walking a balance beam, increasing attention span or reducing temper tantrums. It will occur whether the child's learning disability is neurological or emotional in origin.

The following is a description of a program that was originally designed to remediate the academic and social difficulties of severely emotionally disturbed children, but which was subsequently found to be equally effective with those children who are traditionally called *learning disabled*.

The Therapeutic Education Center in the San Francisco Unified School District began operation in October, 1969, as an ESEA Title III Project. It was designed to serve the educational needs of twenty "severely emotionally disturbed" children between the ages of six and nine who had been unable to function socially or academically in ordinary public-school environments. The program was housed in a private residential facility designed to meet the needs of adolescent girls having difficulty in the community. It was, however, maintained completely as a separate unit from any other program in the facility.

Three separate self-contained classrooms were maintained, organized chiefly on the basis of age groupings, each with six to seven students, a teacher, and a teacher's aid. One additional aid was included on the staff in order to deal with the highly individualized needs of these severely disabled children. In addition to the teaching and teaching-assistant staff, the center included a director as well as a part-time social worker. Even though a token economy system was utilized during a large part of the first year, in which the child could obtain concrete prizes, such as edibles and toys, the program moved away from this type of reinforcement system as quickly as possible and attempted to replace these reinforcers with those normally found in the natural environment, such as free time and curriculum choices.

Psychiatric diagnostic formulations on the twenty children who were in the program during the first year's operation are shown in *Table 1*. These diagnoses were determined before the children entered the program. It should be mentioned that it was our impression that some of the most severely disabled children in the program were among those who had, at that time, no formal diagnosis whatsoever.

A count was also made of the number of times specific behaviors were mentioned by the referral source in the reports on the children who were referred and accepted into the program. *Table 2* presents the frequency of the listing of such behaviors.

TABLE 1

Number of Pupils	Psychiatric Diagnosis
9	None
2	Adjustment reaction of childhood with conduct disturbance
1	Severe behavior disturbance with chronic anxiety
2	Autistic
2	Schizophrenic
2	Schizophrenic personality with neurotic traits
1	Schizoid
1	Unable to determine

TABLE 2

Number of Pupils	Behavior
16	Immature
10	Hyperactive
9	Aggressive with peers
9	Short attention span
8	Withdrawn
7	Aggressive with adults
6	Temper tantrums
5	Destructive
4	Impulsive
4	Limited speech
2	Self-mutilating
2	Stereotype motor activity

It became immediately apparent that a majority of the children included in the program evidenced many of those symptoms suggested by A. A. Strauss and his associates, and further delineated by Schwalb et al., as indicative of brain damage or minimal cerebral dysfunction.[1] Schwalb suggests that a diagnosis of minimal brain damage or minimal brain dysfunction is based on a behavioral-symptom complex consisting of hyperactivity, impulsivity, short attention span, perseveration, near normal, normal, or above normal IQ, specific learning problems such as visual-perceptual problems, poor auditory discrimination, memory problems, mixed laterality and/or right-left disorientation, and coordination problems particularly in tasks requiring fine and rapid motor coordination.[2]

Upon closer examination, five of the twenty children included in this program, though originally referred because of severe emotional disturbance, evidence a sufficient number of the symptoms to allow them to be designated as children with some form of neurologically based learning disorder. Three of the twenty children had been placed in special programs for neurologically handicapped children prior to entry into the Therapeutic Education Center program.

The major objectives of the Therapeutic Education Center program were (1) to decrease the frequency of those behaviors that appeared to get the child in trouble within the normal environment and to increase the frequency of those behaviors felt to be desirable within that same environment, and (2) to increase his academic skills (reading, spelling, and arithmetic) to the point where the child would approximate grade level upon his return to the regular school program.

Essentially, the Therapeutic Education Center program provided a behavior-modification framework and, more specifically, a precision-teaching framework that combined a carefully programed curriculum and a contingent environment, within which the consequences for behaviors and academic skills were made apparent and readily available to the child for specific behaviors. Activities within the program were as follows:

- Two sets of parallel contingency operations: (1) those that were activated when it became necessary to manage an unacceptable behavior; and (2) those in continuous use for the purpose of positively reinforcing acceptable social behaviors and academic skills.

- Individualized step-by-step programing to promote change in both social behavior and academic-skill attainment.

- Precision measurement projects designed to: (1) measure the frequency with which given behaviors occurred within a defined parameter; (2) record the frequency of those behaviors during a program designed to promote change; (3) determine whether or not change had taken place and, if not; (4) make further change.

The approach to learning was individualized and progressed through the following framework:

- The teacher's assessment of the child's level of functioning.
- Sequential academic programing, which started at the child's achievement level and progressed to the next level of complexity on the basis of an 80 percent-accuracy criterion.
- One-to-one and/or small group learning situation.

Even though a behavioral framework was established at the beginning of the program, the actual initiation of the precision teaching and management projects was somewhat slow in getting started during the first year. The following is a summary of those projects that were initiated and carried on during the period from February 1 through June 15, 1970.*

DURING THIS period, 122 individual precision projects were established in our work with the twenty children who participated in the center program. The bulk of these projects were academic in na-

---

*For a more complete description of precision charting techniques, see Bradfield, "Precision Teaching: A Useful Technology for Teachers," Section I, Chapter 3, pp. 31-39.

ture, and this was not a chance occurrence; it was felt by the staff that the preferred way to deal with many of the behavior problems that were occurring was via the development of academic skills. In this way we attempted to develop positive behaviors that were incompatible with those negative behaviors that frequently caused the child to get into trouble in the normal environment. For example, if one of Johnny's problems was that he continually got out of his seat, we might find it more appropriate to pay Johnny off, so to speak, or to reward Johnny for doing arithmetic problems (which required that he remain in his seat). By so doing, we managed to accomplish two purposes with one project; first, to develop academic skills, and second, to decelerate the frequency of a behavior that normally caused the child a great deal of social difficulty. In this way, we not only obtained two behaviors for the price of one, we were also able to pay a great deal of attention to the positive aspects of the child's growth rather than continually focusing upon those negative behaviors which, in many cases, had existed for a long time and often received a great deal of attention. It should be pointed out that this may well have provided reinforcement for the negative behaviors, about which we have long been concerned. This does not mean, however, that we did not set up specific behavior projects — we did. Of the 122 projects, twelve were behavior-deceleration projects, that is, projects specifically designed to decrease or decelerate the frequency with which certain "undesirable" behaviors occurred over time. Talking out in class, getting out of seat, and hitting other children are examples of such behaviors.

Eight behavior-acceleration projects were initiated, involving those behaviors that the staff felt needed to be increased in frequency in individual children. These were primarily social-interaction skills and involved, for the most part, increasing conversational skills of the children with their peers and the staff.

In addition, ten special behavior projects were maintained for a ten-week period from February through May, 1970 with five children who evidenced aggressive behaviors during the recess periods. The remaining 92 projects focused upon the acceleration of academic skills in reading, mathematics, and language. The results of these projects can be seen in *Tables 3* through *9*. In addition, *Wide Range Achievement Tests* were administered to each child upon entry into the program, and again at the end of the school year.[3] Results of these tests will be discussed later in this paper.

AN EXAMINATION of *Tables 3* through *9* reflects some very interesting similarities as well as differences. When we compare the results from the five children designated as learning disabled with results from the total group, we find two immediately apparent differences. First, in the projects that involved development of social behaviors, we find that even though there were twelve behavior-acceleration projects designed to increase the rate at which certain positive social behaviors were occurring, not one of these twelve projects involved any of the children designated as learning disabled. However, on the eight behavior-deceleration projects designed to decrease the rate at which certain undesirable social behaviors were occurring, seven of these eight focused upon behaviors of those children designated as learning disabled. This at least raises the possibility that the learning-disabled child presented more clearly defined negative social behaviors that the staff felt were in need of modification. This was true even though, at the time these projects were initiated and maintained, absolutely no differential diagnosis of learning disability versus emotional disturbance had been made by the staff.

The second obvious difference was in the area of the academic projects. All three of the writing projects that were initiated involved the learning-disabled children, while three of the five language projects involved these children. This would appear to be somewhat disproportionate since the population that we have defined as learning disabled involves only 25 percent of the total population in the program. However, this finding does not appear to be unusual in view of the fact that perceptual-motor and language problems have been clearly defined as areas in which the learning-disabled child frequently manifests specific difficulty. Interestingly enough, projects developed on children who seem to have problems of attention do not suggest that this group was different in behavior, in that exactly 25 percent of the attention projects involved learning-disabled children, while the other 75 percent involved the balance of the children in the program. The balance of the project data would also suggest that the learning-disability children were remarkably similar to the rest of the children in their response to precision projects.

Tables 3A and *3B* present a direct comparison of the number of days it took before the effects of a specific intervention procedure were noted in terms of a change in frequency of a specific behavior rate. In other words, these tables tell us how long it took us to *begin* to modify the behavior of concern. For example, in *Table 3A* we see that, for the total population, the projects indicated that it took from one to five days to begin to see a change in the reading skill upon which the project focused, with the middle number of days required being only one. *Table 3B* shows the same data for those projects involving learning-disability children. In this case it took from two to three days to begin altering behavior, with a middle number of days of two. In the area of mathematics, with the total population, it took from one to three days to begin to see the effect of the change on math skill behavior, with a middle number of days of one, while for the learning-disability group it took one day for a change to begin to have an effect.

Tables 4A and *4B* present the acceleration rates for the specific projects for both the total population and for the learning-disability children. In the area of reading, we find that the acceleration rate of the total group in this particular skill ranged from 0 to 2.3, with a middle acceleration rate of 1.6. This is simply to say that the pro-

TABLE 3A
Days Before Behavior Begins Modifying
Total Population

	Range	Middle
Behavior Acceleration	1-40 (2 failures)	1
Behavior Deceleration	1-6	1
Reading	1-5	1
Math	1-3	1
Writing	1-5	1
Language	1 - Unsuccessful	Unsuccessful
Attention	1-15	1
Special Behavior	1	1

TABLE 3B
Days Before Behavior Begins Modifying
Learning-Disabled Children

	Number of Projects	Range	Middle
Behavior Acceleration	0	–	–
Behavior Deceleration	7	1-5	1
Reading	4	2-3	2
Math	11	1-1	1
Writing	3	1-5	1
Language	3	1-Unsuccessful	Unsuccessful
Attention	2	?	1
Special Behavior	2	1	1

jects multiplied the group's reading rate at a particular difficulty level by an average multiple of 1.6 per week. For the learning-disability children, we find that the acceleration rate for reading ranged from 1.6 to 2.0, with a middle acceleration rate of 1.8. In other words, the learning-disability children increased their reading rates at a specific difficulty level by an average of 1.8 per week.

This does not mean that all children were working at the same difficulty level. It simply means that at whatever difficulty level individual children were working, we were able to increase the rate at which they were able to perform that particular skill by the multiples indicated. We were then able to designate a particular proficiency level that had to be reached before we changed the curriculum to a more difficult performance requirement.

TABLE 4A

Acceleration Rates
Movements Per Minute Per Week
Total Population

	Range	Middle
Behavior Acceleration	0 - 5.0	1.5
Behavior Deceleration	1.4 - 3.2	2.0
Reading	0 - 2.3	1.6
Math	0 - 5.0	1.6
Writing	1.4 - 3.0	1.6
Language	0 - 1.1	0
Attention	0 - 2.0	1.3

TABLE 4B

Acceleration Rates
Movements Per Minute Per Week
Learning-Disabled Children

	Range	Middle
Behavior Acceleration	—	—
Behavior Deceleration	1.4 - 3.0	2.0
Reading	1.6 - 2.0	1.8
Math	1.3 - 2.6	1.6
Writing	1.4 - 3.0	1.6
Language	0 - 1.1	0
Attention	?	?

TABLE 5A
Error Deceleration
Total Population

	Range	Middle
Reading	1.5 - 4.0	2.3
Math	1.4 - 10	2.6
Attention	1.5 - 1.8	1.5

TABLE 5B
Error Deceleration
Learning-Disabled Children

	Range	Middle
Reading	1.5 - 1.8	1.8
Math	1.8 - 4.5	1.8
Attention	?	?

Examination of *Tables 5A* and *5B* provides a comparison between the total group and the learning-disability children with regard to the rates at which we were able to decelerate the errors that they were making in their specific skill subjects at their individual difficulty levels. By maintaining both projects on rates of correct performance and rates of error performance, we were able to see that the child eventually obtained a 90 percent ratio of correct responses to error responses, as well as requiring that he reach a particular frequency of responses per minute.

Tables 6A and *6B* present the comparison of the overall time factor for the precision projects for both the total and learning disability groups. Here again, though we find individual variations, these do not appear to be significant.

Tables 7A and *7B* present the number of minutes per day devoted to the measurement of the specific behaviors noted. For example, in *Table 7A* we find that the middle number of minutes devoted to reading projects was one. This simply means that the average measurement of the child's reading skill per day required one minute of time. This does not mean that only one minute per day was devoted to reading.

TABLE 6A

Project Time in Weeks
Total Population

	Number of Projects	Range	Middle
Behavior Acceleration	12	7-15	9
Behavior Deceleration	8	2-18	5
Reading	20	5-18	13
Math	56	2-25	18
Writing	3	6-13	11
Language	5	7-9	8
Attention	8	9-16	12
Special Behavior	10	12	12

TABLE 6B

Project Time in Weeks
Learning-Disabled Children

	Number of Projects	Range	Middle
Behavior Acceleration	0	—	—
Behavior Deceleration	7	4-12	9
Reading	4	5-14	10
Math	11	4-20	9
Writing	3	6-13	11
Language	3	7-9	8
Attention	2	?	?
Special Behavior	4	12	12

TABLE 7A

Project Time: Minutes Per Day Per Project
Total Population

	Range	Middle
Behavior Acceleration	5 - 60	10
Behavior Deceleration	10 - 120	10
Reading	1 - 5	1
Math	1 - 5	3
Writing	1 - 5	1
Language	5 - 10	10
Attention	1 - 5	5
Special Behavior	10	10

TABLE 7B

Project Time: Minutes Per Day Per Project
Learning-Disabled Children

	Range	Middle
Behavior Acceleration	–	–
Behavior Deceleration	10 - 120	10
Reading	1	1
Math	1 - 5	3
Writing	1 - 5	1
Language	5 - 10	10
Attention	–	–
Special Behavior	10	10

Tables 8A and 8B reflect the number of changes made per project for both the total population and the learning-disability children, and the percentage of these changes that involved antecedent conditions (curriculum), and the percentage that involved subsequent conditions (reinforcement). Changes were made when the child reached a particular proficiency level that we felt was necessary before a more difficult requirement was established. For example, it might be required that Johnny show that he was able to solve single-digit addition problems at a rate of ten problems per minute, with only one error per minute before we moved him to double-digit addition problems. In this way we allowed the child's behavior to guide us in curriculum change rather than making the change without appropriate feedback.

TABLE 8A
Number of Changes Per Project
Total Population

	Range	% Antecedent	% Subsequent
Behavior Acceleration	1-4	42	58
Behavior Deceleration	0-7	36	64
Reading	4-10	89	11
Math	0-12	75	25
Writing	2-5	90	10
Language	0-1	50	50
Attention	1-7	63	37

TABLE 8B
Number of Changes Per Project
Learning-Disabled Children

	Changes	% Antecedent	% Subsequent
Behavior Acceleration	—	—	—
Behavior Deceleration	1-6	40	60
Reading	3-10	82	18
Math	2-8	70	30
Writing	2-5	90	10
Language	1-3	70	30
Attention	2-4	75	25

Table 9 reflects the results of ten special behavior projects that were initiated to reduce the frequency of aggressive behaviors on the playground during recess and lunch periods. Five children were in-

TABLE 9

Frequency of Aggressive Hitting Behaviors on the Playground

CHILD HITS OTHERS

Child	Hitting Rate Before Consequence	Decel. Rate Per Week Before Cons.	Rate After "No Bars" Consequence	Change To Small Playground	Return To Large Playground
A	.4*	0	0	.3	0
B	.5 to .2	1.5	0	.2	0
C	.35	0	0	0	0
D	.5	0	0	.2	0
E	.4 to .2	1.6	0	.1	0

OTHERS HIT CHILD

Child	Hitting Rate Before Consequence	Decel. Rate Per Week Before Cons.	Rate After "No Bars" Consequence	Change To Small Playground	Return To Large Playground
A	.7	0	0	1.0	0
B	.5	0	0	.4	0
C	.2	0	0	0	0
D	0	0	0	.1	0
E	0	0	0	.2	0

*.4 = hitting at rate of four times every ten minutes.

volved, two of whom were learning-disability children, namely *child A* and *child B*. We had observed a high rate of hitting behavior during recess time; for example, column one in *Table 9* shows that *child A* hit other children at the rate of four times every ten minutes, and so forth. Columns one and two reflect the rates of hitting prior to the establishment of a special consequence, while column two reflects the rate at which the behaviors were decelerating under the normal conditions prevailing at that time. Column three reflects the hitting rate after an aversive consequence was established by refusing to allow the children to play on the bars if they hit anyone. As can be readily seen, hitting stopped immediately in all five cases. Column four reflects an interesting situation. It became necessary, for a brief period of time, to move from a very large playground, where the children could, if necessary, avoid one another, which facilitated the reduction of hitting behaviors. Upon change to a playground approximately one third the size of the larger playground, we found that hitting behaviors again developed, though not at the rates at which they had previously occurred. Upon return to the large playground, we found that hitting behaviors again disappeared. It is important to note here that these modifications occurred in all cases, whether the child was categorized in our data as learning disabled or emotionally disturbed.

Finally, in addition to the behavior projects, an attempt was made to complete a *Wide Range Achievement Test* on each child upon his entry into the program, and again in May of the school year. Since this was the first year of the project, many of the children came later in the year, and had been with us only a few months by the end of that school year. As a result, we have broken down the test results into progress per month during the ten-month school year. The concept of grade level implies that during the ten-month school year, the child will grow one grade level, on the average. Therefore, in *Table 10*, the figures represent months of academic skill growth per month. This means, then, that for the total population, the average growth per month was one month gain in reading skills, .8 of a month gain in spelling skills, and 1.3 months gain in arithmetic skills. For the learning-disability children there was a gain of .9 of a month growth in reading skills per month, .8 of a month growth in spelling skills per month, and .8 of a month growth in arithmetic skills per month.

TABLE 10
Monthly Gain in Academic Skills

	Reading	Spelling	Arithmetic
Total Pupil Population	1.0	.8	1.3
Learning-Disabled Children	.9	.8	.8

IN ORDER TO more clearly demonstrate the precision-teaching approach to children in this project, let us look at one particular child within the learning-disability group. This eight-year-old girl entered the project from a special education program for educationally handicapped children outside the San Francisco school district. At the time of entry into the program, she presented a majority of symptoms mentioned previously that suggest a neurologically based learning disability: she evidenced poor perceptual-motor skills, poor motor coordination, poor memory, bizarre behavior, and she was extremely hyperactive. On the *Wide Range Achievement Test* she obtained a reading score of 1.1, a spelling score of 1.0, and an arithmetic score of .9. At the time of entry she made loud and disruptive noises in the classroom at the rate of approximately 1.5 per minute and was out of her seat approximately three times every ten minutes, or once every three minutes. It was determined by the staff that before any academic skills could be worked on effectively, it would be necessary to gain behavior control of this child, and a hierarchy of priorities was established. Two projects were initiated immediately that focused on reducing the frequency of occurrence of out-of-seat behaviors and noise episodes. *Charts 1* and *2* show the results of these projects. Within a period of four weeks, out-of-seat behaviors had been reduced to zero during the entire morning period in class. In this case we did not ignore the behavior as one might think would be advisable. Instead, we simply placed the child back in her seat as soon as she left it, with instructions for her to remain there. The results suggest that this was sufficient.

With regard to the noise episodes, an examination of the chart will show that we initially asked the child to be quiet for one minute at a time, and if she was successful in achieving this one minute of quiet, she was then given one minute of free time to do anything she pleased. Through a series of four changes, the time requirement for being quiet was extended to ten minutes in exchange for one minute of free time. At this time the child showed some regression in the frequency of noise behaviors. It is interesting to note that the increase in noise behavior occurred at the same time as medication was prescribed, and at this time an aversive consequence was established, in which the child was no longer given free time but instead had a token taken away for talking out or making noise. At this point the frequency of the behavior decelerated to zero.

Charts 3 and *4* show that specific academic projects were not initiated until after the children had returned from Easter vacation and this child's social behavior charts indicated that both her out-of-seat and noise behaviors had been reduced to a point where such projects would be effective. At that time, two projects were initiated: an arithmetic project, which focused upon her ability to do simple addition problems, and a reading project, which utilized the Dolch word list (Garrard Publishing Company, Champaign, Illinois).

Charts 3, 4, 5 and *6* show the results of these academic projects. We now had a very desirable situation. The child had an opportunity to be reinforced or rewarded for engaging in academic skill-producing behaviors that were incompatible with the undesirable social behaviors in which she had engaged previously. In other words, she could

161

CHART 1

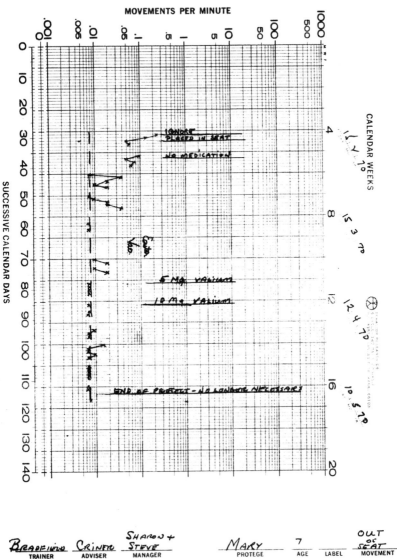

MOVEMENTS PER MINUTE

CALENDAR WEEKS

SUCCESSIVE CALENDAR DAYS

IGNORE
PLACED IN SEAT

NO MEDICATION

5 MG VALIUM

10 Mg VALIUM

END OF PROJECT - NO LONGER NECESSARY

BRADFIELD	CRINITO	SHARON + STEVE	MARY	7		OUT OF SEAT
TRAINER	ADVISER	MANAGER	PROTEGE	AGE	LABEL	MOVEMENT

CHART 2

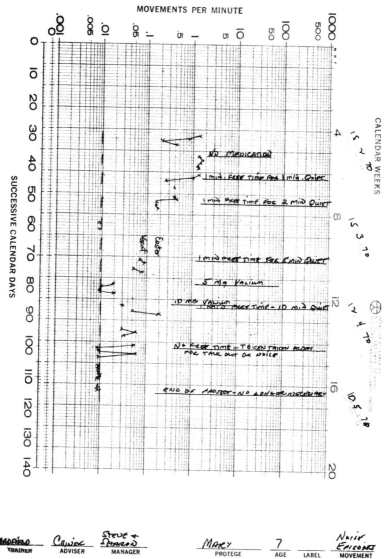

MOVEMENTS PER MINUTE

SUCCESSIVE CALENDAR DAYS

CALENDAR WEEKS

NO MEDICATION

1 min. FREE TIME FOR 1 min. QUIET

1 min FREE TIME FOR 2 min QUIET

Easter

1 min FREE TIME FOR 5 min QUIET

5 Mg VALIUM

10 MG VALIUM FREE TIME - 10 min QUIET

N° FREE TIME - TOKEN TAKEN AWAY FOR TALK OUT OR NOISE

END OF PROJECT - NO LONGER NECESSARY

BRADFIELD   CRUSER   STEVE +
                               SHARON
TRAINER   ADVISER   MANAGER

MARY   7   Noisy
                                      EPISODES
PROTEGE   AGE   LABEL   MOVEMENT

CHART 3

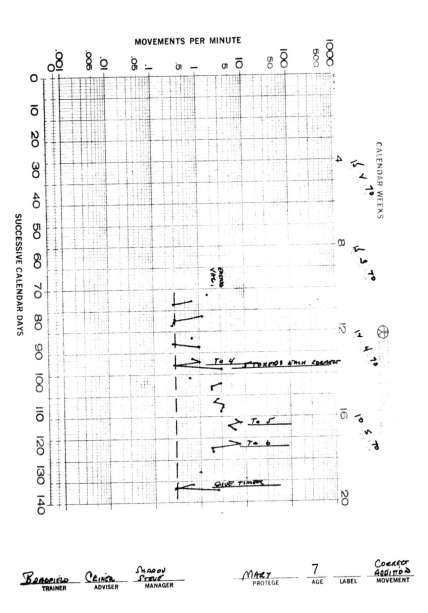

MOVEMENTS PER MINUTE

SUCCESSIVE CALENDAR DAYS

CALENDAR WEEKS

BRADFIELD
TRAINER

CRINER
ADVISER

SHARON
STEVE
MANAGER

MARY
PROTEGE

7
AGE

LABEL

CORRECT
ADDITION
MOVEMENT

CHART 4

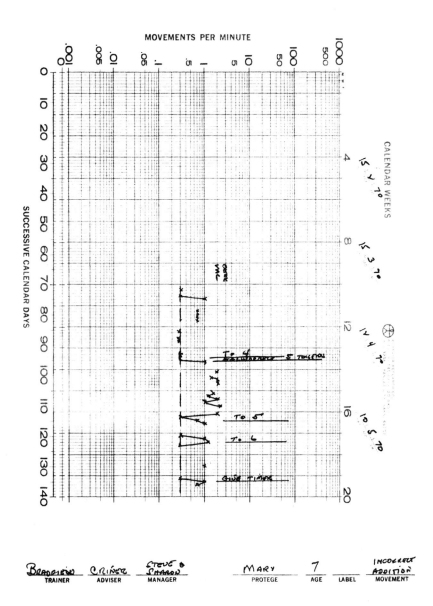

BRADFIELD   C. CLINER   STEVE &   MARY   7   INCORRECT
     SHARON   ADDITION
TRAINER   ADVISER   MANAGER   PROTEGE   AGE   LABEL   MOVEMENT

CHART 5

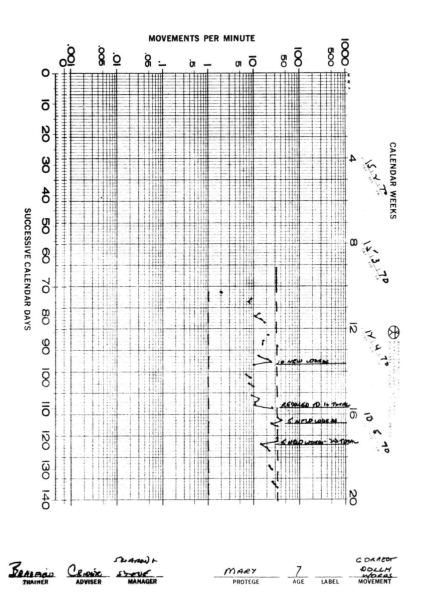

CHART 6

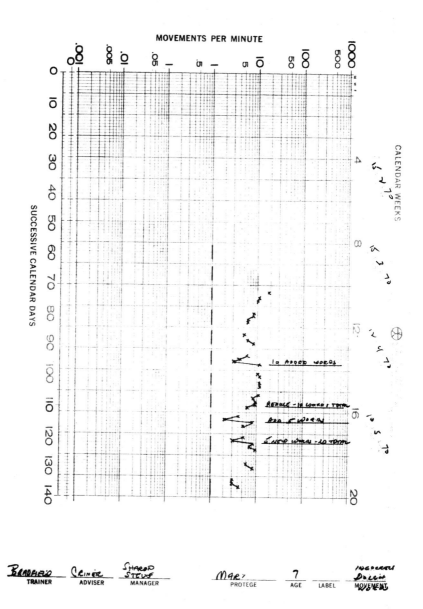

not do her arithmetic problems and receive rewards for doing such problems if she was out of her seat. Planning projects in this way helps not only to build new skills but frequently helps to hold previously high-frequency negative behaviors at a very low rate. Hence, new learning.

DISCUSSION

An examination of the results just presented would seem to suggest the following:

1. Though there may well be identifiable behavioral differences between those children defined as severely emotionally disturbed and those children with minimal brain dysfunction, or neurologically based learning disabilities, these children are still more alike than different. Behavioral differences seem indicated by the following:

- In this program there was a preponderance of behavior deceleration projects for the learning-disabilities group as opposed to behavior acceleration projects for the balance of the project population. It is important to recognize that behavior deceleration projects focus primarily upon "acting out" types of behavior of either an aggressive or hyperactive nature. Behavior acceleration projects tended to focus upon increasing the rate of interaction behaviors and promoting socialized peer interaction. It will be recalled that no behavior acceleration projects were initiated on the group defined as having learning disabilities.

- A difference was noted in the number of projects that focused upon those academic areas that emphasized perceptual-motor responses, that is, writing and language. It will again be recalled that all writing projects and three of the five language projects were maintained on the children in the learning-disabilities group. It should be reemphasized that no formal differential diagnosis was utilized by the staff in determining those projects which should be initiated but rather that the projects were based on teacher evaluation of the specific behavioral needs, both academic and social, of the child in question. In other words, the projects were designed for individual children on the basis of their behaviors rather than on the basis of the category to which they had been assigned.

2. In all other areas the projects were essentially the same. Precision projects in reading, arithmetic, increasing attention span, and the reduction of aggressive behavior all showed highly similar results. In almost every case, regardless of the skill or behavior area, all the children in the project responded to precise behavioral management as had been expected. This suggestion of similarity between the two groups is not surprising when we consider that an evaluation of the available literature on both the emotionally disturbed child and the learning-disabled child suggest that they do, in fact, share many of the same "symptoms," and that it is only when a large number of these symptoms can be combined in a single child

that he is placed within a particular category. In this regard, it should be mentioned that even though, for the purposes of research, we have selected those five children who can reasonably fall within the definition of learning disabilities, all of the children in the project manifested one or more of these same symptoms. An example of this is found in the fact that eight of the projects were initiated to increase attention span of children in the program. Only two of these projects were initiated on children who were clearly defined as learning disabled. It should further be noted that no significant difference seemed to exist in the attention projects of the learning-disability group as compared to the total population.

3. We strongly feel that further attempts to delineate specific educational programs for particular categories of children is not only impractical but totally unnecessary. At the center we have utilized a system of individualized precision programing based on an analysis of specific behaviors. During our initial year of operation these methods proved equally successful with all of the children in the project, whatever their categorical placement. Precision teaching, the methodological approach upon which our program is based, requires the precise definition of specific behaviors of concern, the arrangement of these behaviors into an individual hierarchy of priorities for each child, the careful delineation of those antecedent and subsequent conditions that might effect a change in these behaviors, continued feedback with regard to the results of our efforts to change the behavior, and the modification of programs on the basis of changes in the child's behavior. We do not need categories to accomplish this purpose; all we need is children.

4. The program is changing as the children change. It is not intended to be a static or rigid attempt to fit the children into our mold, but rather to allow us to respond to changes in the children. As the children have gained behavioral controls, we have changed our program to take advantage of that improved control. In planning for the center's second year of operation, it has been not only possible but necessary to adapt the original program. The reinforcement system that was originally used stressed immediate and material reinforcement; it has been modified to include rewards that are increasingly symbolic and delayed, and the social reinforcement of adult approbation has increased in significance. As a result of the gains made by the children in behavior controls, it now becomes necessary to provide additional opportunities for social growth, together with the possibilities of enriching academic opportunities as the children are able to utilize more and different methods of instruction. For example, with the children's increased ability to function in activity groups, the center is now able to include in the second year's programing an organized physical education unit. This functions as a further opportunity to expand functioning in groups as a way of increasing the pupils' social aptitudes, while at the same time it is geared to the development of basic motor skills. Another example of program adaptation is in the move from highly individualized instruc-

tion with a low level of stimulation to a curriculum that now includes programing which takes place in small groups with a lot of shouting and clapping. The children involved in such programs now have sufficient behavioral controls to "come down" from the excitement engendered by such group participation. Changes in the curriculum aspects of the program are a requisite of the precision teaching program, and these continuing changes will be assessed by individual projects designed to measure behavior change in the child. It is these projects that will tell us which of our curricular changes are appropriate.

We do not know what the long-range results of this project will be, and we can only rely on information that is currently available. In addition to the data cited above, we have currently returned two of the original twenty children to regular classrooms in the public school system. Current plans call for the return of four more of the original children if their existing rates of progress continue within the next few months. Beyond this, we can only speculate. Results obtained during the coming two years may help us further clarify and delineate the effectiveness of precision teaching with both severely emotionally disturbed and learning-disability children.

SUMMARY

In a program designed for severely emotionally disturbed children, one-fourth of the pupil population fitted the learning-disability classification, and all of the pupils manifested at least one or more of the characteristics that typify the learning-disabilities child. The methods utilized at the Therapeutic Education Center were effective with both groups. Many emotionally disturbed children appear to have learning disabilities, and many children with learning disabilities appear to evidence emotionally disturbed behaviors. Insofar as either category is effective in providing a base for educational programing, the question is raised as to whether or not these are but artificial separations. Precision teaching projects were effective in establishing desired behaviors of both an academic and social nature, in both groups of children.

NOTES

1. A. A. Strauss and L. Lehtinen, *Psychopathology and Education of the Brain-Injured Child*, Vol. 1 (New York, N.Y.: Grune and Stratton, 1947); A. A. Strauss and N. Kephart, *Psychopathology and Education of the Brain-Injured Child*, Vol. 2 (New York, N.Y.: Grune and Stratton, 1955); Eugene Schwalb et al., "Child with Brain Dysfunction," *Journal of Learning Disabilities*, 2, No. 4 (April 1969), 182-188.

2. Schwab et al., "Child with Brain Dysfunction."

3. J. Jastak and S. Bijou, *Wide Range Achievement Tests* (New York, N. Y.: The Psychological Corporation, 1946-1965).

CONTRIBUTORS

Alfred A. Artuso, Ed.D.: Superintendent of Schools, Santa Monica, California.

Cedric Benson, M.S.: Director, West Suburban Association for Special Education, Oak Park, Illinois.

Martha E. Bernal, Ph.D.: Associate Professor, Department of Psychology, University of Denver, Colorado.

Robert H. Bradfield, Ph.D.: Associate Professor, Department of Special Education, San Francisco State College, California.

Marilyn Clark, M.S.: Learning Specialist, Special Services, Shawnee Mission Public Schools, Kansas.

Jane Criner, M.S.W.: Project Director, Teacher Education Center, San Francisco Unified School District, California.

Burl B. Gray, Ph.D.: Director of Research-Speech Pathology, Behavioral Sciences Institute, Monterey, California.

Norris G. Haring, Ed.D.: Director, Experimental Education Unit, Child Development and Mental Retardation Center; Professor of Education and Lecturer in Pediatrics; University of Washington, Seattle.

Frank M. Hewett, Ph.D.: Professor of Education and Psychiatry; Chairman, Special Education; University of California, Los Angeles.

Richard Kothera, Ed.D.: Superintendent of Schools, Roseland District 92, Shawnee Mission, Kansas.

Harold P. Kunzelmann: Supervisor, Mental Retardation Programs, Department of Special Education, State of Washington.

Thomas C. Lovitt, Ed.D.: Associate Professor, College of Education, Experimental Education Unit, University of Washington, Seattle.

Garry L. Martin, Ph.D.: Assistant Professor of Psychology, University of Manitoba, Winnipeg, Canada.